CONTENTS

MEAL PLANNING MADE EASY

Your *No Time To Cook 6 Ingredients or Less cookbook is filled with fabulous recipes for those with little time to spend in the kitchen. All the recipes included can be made with six ingredients or less (not including salt, pepper or water). You'll be delighted at how flavor-packed these recipes are! From appetizers and salads to main dishes and desserts, these dishes call for easy-to-find ingredients. Almost every recipe can be made in thirty minutes or less. This will allow you more time to spend with your family, while still serving them delicious homemade meals.*

Even with a busy schedule you can still have time to prepare special meals using the recipes included here. These recipes are suitable for a family gathering, casual get-together or weeknight meal. Try using some of our menu ideas or create your own to make your evening meals enjoyable.

HEARTY WINTER MEAL
Warm up on a cold winter night with a hearty home-cooked meal.

SUMMER EVENING PICNIC
Enjoy the fresh breezes of a summer evening while you have a picnic in your backyard!

MEXICAN FIESTA
Spice up your meal with these south-of-the-border flavors!

Simple Starters

Chunky Pecan and Beef Dip (page 5)

INDEX

ARTICHOKE CROSTINI

1 jar (6 ounces) marinated artichoke hearts, drained and chopped
3 green onions, chopped
5 tablespoons grated Parmesan cheese, divided
2 tablespoons mayonnaise
12 slices French bread (½ inch thick)

1. Preheat broiler. Combine artichokes, green onions, 3 tablespoons cheese and mayonnaise in small bowl; mix well.

2. Arrange bread slices on baking sheet. Broil 4 to 5 inches from heat source 2 to 3 minutes on each side or until lightly browned.

3. Remove baking sheet from broiler. Spoon about 1 tablespoon artichoke mixture on each bread slice and sprinkle with

remaining 2 tablespoons cheese. Broil 1 to 2 minutes or until cheese is melted and lightly browned. *Makes 4 servings*

Prep and cook time: 25 minutes

Nutrients per serving: Calories: 324, Total Fat: 14 g, Protein: 10 g, Carbohydrate: 43 g, Cholesterol: 9 mg, Sodium: 758 mg, Dietary Fiber: trace
Dietary Exchanges: Vegetable: 1, Bread: 2½, Fat: 2½

Serve It With Style!
Garnish with red bell pepper, if desired.

EASY ITALIAN NO-BAKE SNACK MIX

3 tablespoons olive oil
1 tablespoon Italian seasoning
1 box (7 ounces) baked crispy snack crackers
4 cups small pretzels
1 can (12 ounces) cocktail peanuts
¼ cup grated Parmesan cheese

1. Combine oil and seasoning in large resealable plastic food storage bag; knead well.

2. Add crackers, pretzels and peanuts. Seal bag; shake gently to coat well with oil mixture. Add grated cheese. Seal bag; shake gently to combine. Snack mix can be stored in bag up to 5 days.

Makes 10 cups

Prep time: 10 minutes

Nutrients per serving (1 cup): Calories: 397, Total Fat: 26 g, Protein: 14 g, Carbohydrate: 33 g, Cholesterol: 2 mg, Sodium: 587 mg, Dietary Fiber: 3 g Dietary Exchanges: Bread: 2, Meat: 1, Fat: 4½

Serve It With Style!

For a change of pace, prepare Easy Italian No-Bake Snack Mix with almonds, cashews or walnuts instead of cocktail peanuts.

Cook's Notes:

Using spice blends is a convenience. Common dried herbs used in Italian seasoning blends are oregano, marjoram, red pepper, basil, rosemary, thyme and sage.

EASY EASEL RECIPES

CHUNKY PECAN AND BEEF DIP

½ **cup pecan pieces**

3 **tablespoons thinly sliced green onions with tops**

1 **package (8 ounces) cream cheese, softened and cut into cubes**

½ **jar (2.2 ounces) dried beef, rinsed in hot water, drained and cut into ¼-inch pieces**

½ **teaspoon dried Italian seasoning**
Bread sticks, pita bread and assorted fresh vegetables for dipping

1. Spray bottom of small saucepan generously with nonstick cooking spray; heat over medium heat until hot. Add pecans and onions; cook over medium heat 3 to 5 minutes or until pecans are toasted and onions are tender.

2. Add ¼ cup hot water and cream cheese to

saucepan; cook over medium-low heat until cheese is melted. Stir in dried beef and Italian seasoning; cook over medium-high heat, stirring constantly, until hot.

3. Spoon into bowl; sprinkle with additional green onion tops, if desired. Serve with dippers. *Makes 8 (3-tablespoon) servings*

Prep and cook time: 18 minutes

Nutrients per serving: Calories: 152, Total Fat: 15 g, Protein: 4 g, Carbohydrate: 2 g, Cholesterol: 35 mg, Sodium: 221 mg, Dietary Fiber: trace
Dietary Exchanges: Meat: ½, Fat: 3

FUDGY BANANA ROCKY ROAD CLUSTERS

2 cups (12 ounces) semisweet chocolate chips
⅓ cup peanut butter
3 cups miniature marshmallows
1 cup unsalted peanuts
1 cup banana chips

1. Place semisweet chocolate chips and peanut butter in large microwavable bowl. Microwave at HIGH 2 minutes or until chips are melted and mixture is smooth, stirring mixture twice.

2. Fold in marshmallows, peanuts and banana chips.

3. Line baking sheets with waxed paper and grease. Drop rounded

tablespoonfuls candy mixture onto prepared baking sheets, refrigerating mixture until firm. Store candy clusters in airtight container in refrigerator.

Makes 2½ to 3 dozen clusters

Prep time: 30 minutes

Nutrients per serving: Calories: 117, Total Fat: 7 g, Protein: 3 g, Carbohydrate: 12 g, Cholesterol: trace, Sodium: 15 mg, Dietary Fiber: 1 g
Dietary Exchanges: Bread: 1, Fat: 1

Cook's Notes:
If you prefer more nuts, use chunky peanut butter when preparing Fudgy Banana Rocky Road Clusters.

PEPPER CHEESE COCKTAIL PUFFS

½ **package (17¼ ounces) frozen puff pastry, thawed**
1 **tablespoon Dijon mustard**
½ **cup (2 ounces) finely shredded Cheddar cheese**
1 **teaspoon cracked black pepper**
1 **egg**

1. Preheat oven to 400°F. Grease baking sheets.

2. Roll out 1 sheet of dough onto well floured surface to 14×10-inch rectangle. Spread half of dough (from 10-inch side) with mustard. Sprinkle with cheese and pepper. Fold dough over filling; roll gently to seal edges.

3. Cut lengthwise into 3 strips; cut each strip diagonally into 1½-inch

pieces. Place on prepared baking sheets. Beat egg and 1 tablespoon water in small bowl; brush on appetizers.

4. Bake appetizers 12 to 15 minutes or until puffed and deep golden brown. Remove from baking sheets to wire rack to cool.

Makes about 20 appetizers

Prep and cook time: 30 minutes

Nutrients per serving (3 puffs): Calories: 283, Total Fat: 19 g, Protein: 6 g, Carbohydrate: 21 g, Cholesterol: 34 mg, Sodium: 390 mg, Dietary Fiber: 0 g Dietary Exchanges: Bread: 1½, Fat: 4

Cook's Notes:
Work quickly and efficiently when using puff pastry. The colder puff pastry is, the better it will puff in the hot oven. Also, this recipe can be easily doubled.

BROWNIE BAKED ALASKAS

2 purchased brownies (2½ inches square)
2 scoops fudge swirl ice cream (or favorite flavor)
⅓ cup semisweet chocolate chips
2 tablespoons light corn syrup or milk
2 egg whites
¼ cup sugar

1. Preheat oven to 500°F. Place brownies on small cookie sheet; top each with scoop of ice cream and place in freezer.

2. Melt chocolate chips in small saucepan over low heat. Stir in corn syrup; set aside and keep warm.

3. Beat egg whites to soft peaks in small bowl. Gradually beat in sugar; continue beating until stiff peaks form. Spread egg white mixture over ice cream and brownies with small spatula (ice cream and brownies should be completely covered with egg white mixture).

4. Bake 2 to 3 minutes or until meringue is golden. Spread chocolate sauce on serving plates; place baked Alaskas over sauce. Serve immediately.   *Makes 2 servings*

Prep and cook time: 17 minutes

Nutrients per serving: Calories: 709, Total Fat: 27 g, Protein: 10 g, Carbohydrate: 117 g, Cholesterol: 39 mg, Sodium: 299 mg, Dietary Fiber: 0 g
Dietary Exchanges: Bread: 7, Fat: 4½

NACHOS OLÉ

1 ½ cups (6 ounces) shredded Monterey Jack cheese

1 ½ cups (6 ounces) shredded Cheddar cheese

1 ½ cups refried beans

6 dozen packaged corn tortilla chips

1 large tomato, seeded and chopped

½ cup pickled jalapeño chilies, thinly sliced

1. Preheat oven to 400°F. Combine cheeses in small bowl.

2. Cook and stir beans in small saucepan over medium heat until hot. Spread 1 teaspoon beans on each tortilla chip. Arrange chips in single layer on 2 to 3 baking sheets. Sprinkle chips evenly with tomato and chilies; sprinkle with cheese mixture.

3. Bake 5 to 8 minutes until cheese is bubbly and melted. *Makes 4 to 6 servings*

Prep and cook time: 20 minutes

Nutrients per serving: Calories: 630, Total Fat: 35 g, Protein: 25 g, Carbohydrate: 52 g, Cholesterol: 83 mg, Sodium: 1927 mg, Dietary Fiber: 7 g
Dietary Exchanges: Bread: 3, Meat: 2, Fat: 6½

Cook's Notes:

Jalapeño chilies are small, dark green Mexican hot peppers. Chilies range from hot to very hot and can be purchased fresh, canned or bottled.

EASY EASEL RECIPES

CUPID CAKES

1 **package (10 ounces) frozen strawberries, thawed**
1 **tablespoon powdered sugar**
½ **cup whipping cream, whipped**
2 **frozen all-butter pound cakes (10.75 ounces each), thawed**
½ **cup strawberry or seedless raspberry preserves**

1. Drain strawberries, reserving 1 tablespoon juice. Discard remaining juice. Gently combine strawberries, reserved juice and powdered sugar with whipped cream; set aside.

2. Cut each cake into 12 slices. Spread 12 slices with about 1½ teaspoons preserves each. Top with remaining slices to make sandwiches, pressing gently to spread preserves to edges. Scrape excess preserves from edges.

Place onto serving plates; top with whipped cream mixture. *Makes 12 servings*

Prep and cook time: 15 minutes

Nutrients per serving: Calories: 278, Total Fat: 14 g, Protein: 3 g, Carbohydrate: 37 g, Cholesterol: 14 mg, Sodium: 207 mg, Dietary Fiber: 1 g
Dietary Exchanges: Fruit: 1, Bread: 1½, Fat: 2½

Serve It With Style!

For an accompaniment, serve Cupid Cakes with your favorite flavored instant coffee.

CURRIED FRUIT DIP

1 cup sour cream
3 tablespoons mango chutney
2 tablespoons unsweetened pineapple
    juice
2 teaspoons honey-Dijon mustard
1 teaspoon curry powder
1 teaspoon grated orange peel

1. Place sour cream in small bowl. Stir in chutney, pineapple juice, mustard, curry and orange peel until well blended.

2. Transfer dip to serving bowl. Serve immediately or cover with plastic wrap and refrigerate until ready to serve.

Makes 1½ cups

Prep time: 10 minutes

SERVING SUGGESTION: *Serve dip with assorted cut-up fresh fruits and vegetables.*

Nutrients per serving (2 tablespoons): Calories: 54, Total Fat: 4 g, Protein: 1 g, Carbohydrate: 4 g, Cholesterol: 9 mg, Sodium: 22 mg, Dietary Fiber: trace Dietary Exchanges: Fat: 1

Cook's Notes:
Curry powder is a blend of up to 20 spices, herbs and seeds. It should be stored airtight to preserve its pungency.

EASY EASEL RECIPES

CRANBERRY CHEESECAKE MUFFINS

1 package (3 ounces) cream cheese, softened
¼ cup sugar, divided
1 cup 2% milk
⅓ cup vegetable oil
1 egg
1 package (15.6 ounces) cranberry quick bread mix

1. Preheat oven to 400°F. Grease 12 muffin cups.

2. Beat cream cheese and 2 tablespoons sugar in small bowl until well blended. Combine milk, oil and egg in large bowl; beat with fork until blended. Stir in quick bread mix just until dry ingredients are moistened.

3. Fill muffin cups ¼ full with batter. Drop 1 teaspoon cream cheese mixture into center of each cup. Spoon remaining batter over cream cheese mixture.

4. Sprinkle batter with remaining 2 tablespoons sugar. Bake 17 to 22 minutes or until golden brown. Cool 5 minutes. Remove from muffin cups to wire rack to cool. *Makes 12 muffins*

Prep and cook time: 30 minutes

Nutrients per serving (1 muffin):
Calories: 251, Total Fat: 10 g,
Protein: 4 g, Carbohydrate: 35 g,
Cholesterol: 27 mg,
Sodium: 187 mg,
Dietary Fiber: 0 g
Dietary Exchanges: Bread: 2½,
Fat: 1½

GARLIC BEAN DIP

4 cloves garlic
1 can (15½ ounces) pinto or black
     beans, rinsed and drained
¼ cup pimiento-stuffed green olives
4½ teaspoons lemon juice
½ teaspoon ground cumin
    Assorted fresh vegetables and crackers

1. Place garlic in food processor; process until minced. Add beans, olives, lemon juice and cumin; process until well blended but not entirely smooth. Serve with vegetables and crackers.

Makes about 1½ cups

Prep time: 10 minutes

*Nutrients per serving
(2 tablespoons): Calories: 42,
Total Fat: 1 g, Protein: 3 g,
Carbohydrate: 7 g,
Cholesterol: 0 mg,
Sodium: 207 mg,
Dietary Fiber: 0 g
Dietary Exchanges: Bread: ½*

CUTTING CORNERS:
To save time, try buying fresh vegetables, such as carrots and celery, already cut up from the produce section of the supermarket.

Cook's Notes:
The spice cumin is widely used in Middle Eastern, Asian and Mediterranean cooking. Cumin is available in seed and ground form and adds a nutty flavor to dishes.

EASY EASEL RECIPES

RASPBERRY NAPOLEONS

¼ **package (5 ounces) refrigerated sugar cookie dough**
1 **container (8 ounces) whipped cream cheese**
½ **cup sifted powdered sugar, divided**
2 **tablespoons Grand Marnier or brandy, divided**
2 **cups fresh or thawed frozen blueberries**
2 **cups sliced fresh or thawed frozen raspberries or strawberries**

1. Roll cookie dough to ¼-inch-thick disc. Cut 4 (3-inch) cookies using cookie cutter; place on nonstick baking sheet. Reroll dough scraps and cut out with 1- or 2-inch cookie cutters. Bake according to package directions.

2. Beat cream cheese, ¼ cup sugar and 1 tablespoon liqueur until smooth; set aside. Combine blueberries, remaining ¼ cup sugar and remaining 1 tablespoon liqueur in food processor or blender; process until smooth. Pour through fine-meshed sieve; discard skins.

3. Place large cookies on serving plates; spoon cream cheese mixture over tops. Arrange smaller cookies and raspberries on top. Spoon blueberry sauce around Napoleons.

Makes 4 servings

Prep and cook time:
25 minutes

Nutrients per serving:
Calories: 517, Total Fat: 29 g,
Protein: 7 g, Carbohydrate: 58 g,
Cholesterol: 73 mg,
Sodium: 342 mg,
Dietary Fiber: 5 g
Dietary Exchanges: Milk: 1,
Fruit: 2, Bread: 1½, Fat: 6

EASY EASEL RECIPES

CARIBBEAN DREAM

¾ **cup vanilla ice cream**
¾ **cup pineapple sherbet**
¾ **cup tropical fruit salad, drained**
¼ **cup frozen banana-orange juice concentrate**
¼ **teaspoon rum-flavored extract**

1. Place ice cream, sherbet, tropical fruit, concentrate and rum extract in blender. Blend on medium speed 1 to 2 minutes or until smooth and well blended.

2. Pour into 2 serving glasses. Serve immediately.

Makes 2 servings

Prep time: 10 minutes

Nutrients per serving:
Calories: 310, Total Fat: 6 g,
Protein: 3 g, Carbohydrate: 64 g,
Cholesterol: 33 mg,
Sodium: 45 mg,
Dietary Fiber: trace
Dietary Exchanges: Bread: 3½,
Fat: 1

Serve It With Style!
Try adding a tablespoon of rum instead of rum extract for a more mature flavor.

LIGHTEN UP:
To reduce the fat, replace vanilla ice cream with reduced-fat or fat-free ice cream or frozen yogurt.

EASY EASEL RECIPES

TROPICAL PASTRIES

1 bag (6 ounces) diced dried tropical
    fruit medley or other diced dried
    fruit mixture
½ cup orange juice
2 cans (8 ounces each) crescent dinner
    rolls
5 tablespoons margarine or butter,
    melted, divided
2 tablespoons packed brown sugar
    Powdered sugar

1. Preheat oven to 375°F. Combine fruit and juice in small microwavable bowl. Cover with vented plastic wrap. Microwave on HIGH 3 to 5 minutes or until juice has been absorbed.

2. While fruit is cooking, unroll dough from 1 can and separate along perforations to form 4 rectangles, about 5×4 inches each. Do not separate dough into triangles. Press diagonal cuts in rectangles to reseal dough. Repeat with remaining can. Brush each rectangle with 1½ teaspoons margarine.

3. Stir brown sugar into fruit. Sprinkle 2 tablespoons fruit mixture horizontally across center of each rectangle. To form, fold bottom edge of dough up over filling; fold in sides, then roll up to completely enclose filling. Place seam sides down on baking sheet. Brush with remaining 1 tablespoon margarine.

4. Bake 12 to 15 minutes or until golden brown. Serve warm or at room temperature. Sprinkle with powdered sugar immediately before serving. *Makes 8 servings*

Prep and cook time: 20 minutes

Nutrients per serving: Calories: 347, Total Fat: 19 g,
Protein: 5 g, Carbohydrate: 42 g, Cholesterol: 0 mg,
Sodium: 579 mg, Dietary Fiber: 2 g
Dietary Exchanges: Fruit: 1, Bread: 2, Fat: 3

STRAWBERRY CHAMPAGNE PUNCH

2 packages (10 ounces each) frozen
    sliced strawberries in syrup, thawed
2 cans (5½ ounces each) apricot or
    peach nectar
¼ cup lemon juice
2 tablespoons honey
2 bottles (750 ml each) champagne or
    sparkling white wine, chilled

Prep time: 15 minutes

*Nutrients per serving: Calories: 160, Total Fat: 0 g,
Protein: 1 g, Carbohydrate: 22 g, Cholesterol: 0 mg,
Sodium: 2 mg, Dietary Fiber: 1 g
Dietary Exchanges: Fruit: 1½, Fat: 1½*

CUTTING CORNERS:
To save time, thaw the strawberries in the
refrigerator the day before using them.

1. Place strawberries with syrup in food
processor; process until smooth.

2. Pour puréed
strawberries into punch
bowl. Stir in apricot
nectar, lemon juice and
honey; blend well.
Refrigerate until serving.

3. To serve, stir
champagne into
strawberry mixture and
pour into glasses.
                Makes 12 servings

EASY EASEL RECIPES

SUMMER PEACH SHORT "CAKES"

6 medium peaches or nectarines, peeled and thinly sliced

⅓ cup sugar

2 tablespoons orange or lemon juice

⅓ cup chocolate-covered toffee pieces

1 container (16 ounces) cream cheese frosting

2 frozen pound cakes (10.75 ounces each)

1. Combine peaches, sugar and orange juice in large bowl. Crush peaches with potato masher or large spoon. Stir well; set aside.

2. Stir toffee into frosting; set aside. Cut pound cakes into ¼-inch slices; discard end pieces. Spread 1 tablespoon frosting mixture on 1 side of cake slice; top with another slice, pressing gently.

Repeat with remaining slices and frosting. Serve 2 cake sandwiches; top with ¼ cup peach mixture.   *Makes about 7 servings*

Prep time: 30 minutes

FOR A SPECIAL TOUCH, CUT EACH CAKE SANDWICH INTO TRIANGLES AND ARRANGE ON SERVING PLATTER IN A STARBURST DESIGN. SPOON PEACH MIXTURE INTO CENTER.

Nutrients per serving: Calories: 720, Total Fat: 31 g, Protein: 6 g, Carbohydrate: 109 g, Cholesterol: 2 mg, Sodium: 508 mg, Dietary Fiber: 1 g
Dietary Exchanges: Bread: 7, Fat: 5

CUTTING CORNERS:
Don't thaw pound cake before slicing—it's easier to slice when it's partially frozen.

SNOWBIRD MOCKTAILS

3 cups pineapple juice
1 can (14 ounces) sweetened condensed
   milk
1 can (6 ounces) frozen orange juice
   concentrate, thawed
½ teaspoon coconut extract
1 bottle (32 ounces) ginger ale, chilled

1. Combine pineapple juice, sweetened
condensed milk, orange juice concentrate
and coconut extract in large pitcher; stir
well. Refrigerate, covered, up to 1 week.

2. To serve, pour ½ cup
pineapple juice mixture
into individual glasses
(over crushed ice, if
desired). Top off each
glass with about ⅓ cup
ginger ale.

Makes 10 servings

Prep time: 10 minutes

*Nutrients per serving: Calories: 228, Total Fat: 4 g,
Protein: 4 g, Carbohydrate: 46 g, Cholesterol: 13 mg,
Sodium: 58 mg, Dietary Fiber: trace
Dietary Exchanges: Milk: 1, Fruit: 2, Fat: ½*

Cook's Notes:

*Store unopened cans of sweetened condensed
milk at room temperature up to 6 months.
Once opened, store in an airtight container in
the refrigerator for up to 5 days.*

EASY EASEL RECIPES

SUNDAE SHORTCAKES

1 cup sugar

⅓ cup thawed frozen orange juice concentrate

3 tablespoons butter or margarine

1 can (17.3 ounces) refrigerated buttermilk biscuits

1 pint frozen vanilla or fruit-flavored yogurt or vanilla ice cream

3 cups fresh or thawed frozen blackberries

1. Combine sugar, orange juice concentrate, ⅓ cup water and butter in small saucepan. Bring to a boil over medium-high heat, stirring constantly, until sugar is melted. Boil gently, uncovered, 5 minutes.

2. Prepare biscuits according to package

directions. Pierce 4 biscuits all over with skewer. Spoon ¼ of sugar mixture over 4 biscuits. Let stand 1 minute. Reserve remaining biscuits for another use.

3. Split biscuits; place bottom halves on serving plates. Spoon yogurt evenly over bottoms; top with blackberries. Drizzle with remaining sugar mixture; top with biscuit tops. *Makes 4 servings*

Prep and cook time: 30 minutes

SERVING SUGGESTION:
Serve with frozen whipped topping.

Nutrients per serving:
Calories: 765, Total Fat: 19 g,
Protein: 10 g,
Carbohydrate: 148 g,
Cholesterol: 25 mg,
Sodium: 1192 mg,
Dietary Fiber: 8 g
Dietary Exchanges: Fruit: 5,
Bread: 5, Fat: 2½

EASY EASEL
RECIPES

PEANUT BUTTER & JELLY SHAKES

1½ **cups vanilla ice cream**
¼ **cup milk**
2 **tablespoons creamy peanut butter**
6 **peanut butter sandwich cookies,**
   coarsely chopped
¼ **cup strawberry preserves**

1. Place ice cream, milk and peanut butter in blender. Blend on medium speed 1 to 2 minutes or until smooth and well blended. Add cookie pieces and blend 10 seconds on low speed. Pour into 2 serving glasses.

2. Place preserves and 1 to 2 teaspoons water in small bowl; stir until smooth. Stir 2 tablespoons preserve mixture into each glass. Serve immediately.

Makes 2 servings

Prep time: 10 minutes

Nutrients per serving: Calories: 571, Total Fat: 28 g, Protein: 12 g, Carbohydrate: 73 g, Cholesterol: 61 mg, Sodium: 278 mg, Dietary Fiber: 1 g Dietary Exchanges: Bread: 5, Fat: 5

Serve It With Style!

For a change of pace, prepare these shakes using different flavors of preserves.

Cook's Notes:

Eat this thick and creamy shake with a spoon for a mouthful of cookies in every bite.

RASPBERRY CHANTILLY PARFAITS

1 **container (8 ounces) vanilla yogurt**
½ **cup sifted powdered sugar**
1 **package (10 ounces) frozen raspberries in light syrup, thawed**
4 **cups thawed frozen whipped topping**
1⅓ **cups crushed oatmeal cookies or low-fat granola cereal**
1⅓ **cups fresh blueberries**

1. Spread yogurt to ½-inch thickness on several layers of paper towels; place 2 layers of paper towels over yogurt. Let stand 15 minutes. Scrape yogurt from paper towels into large bowl using rubber spatula. Stir in sugar.

2. Place raspberries in food processor or blender; process until smooth. Pour through fine-meshed sieve into bowl;

press raspberries with back of spoon against sides of sieve to squeeze out liquid. Discard seeds. Stir into yogurt mixture. Fold in whipped topping.

3. Spoon half of yogurt mixture into 4 (8- to 12-ounce) stemmed glasses; sprinkle with half of crushed cookies and blueberries. Repeat layers. Serve immediately or cover and refrigerate up to 2 hours.

Makes 4 servings

Prep and cook time: 25 minutes

FOR A SPECIAL TOUCH, GARNISH WITH FRESH MINT LEAVES AND ADDITIONAL BLUEBERRIES.

Nutrients per serving:
Calories: 567, Total Fat: 23 g,
Protein: 7 g, Carbohydrate: 86 g,
Cholesterol: 8 mg,
Sodium: 114 mg,
Dietary Fiber: 5 g
Dietary Exchanges: Milk: 1,
Fruit: 4, Bread: 2, Fat: 4

EASY EASEL RECIPES

Salads & Soups

Beef & Blue Cheese Salad (page 16)

PATRIOTIC PARFAITS

**4 containers (3½ ounces each) tapioca
  pudding, chilled**
8 vanilla sandwich cookies, crumbled
¾ cup fresh blueberries
**½ cup strawberry ice cream topping,
  chilled**

1. Place half of pudding container into each
of 4 (6- to 8-ounce) parfait glasses; top
evenly with half of cookies. Sprinkle
2 tablespoons blueberries over each parfait.
Repeat layer with remaining pudding and
cookies.

2. Spoon 2 tablespoons
strawberry topping and
1 tablespoon blueberries
over cookies in each
parfait.

Makes 4 servings

Prep time: 15 minutes

SERVING SUGGESTION: *Serve additional
vanilla sandwich cookies with Patriotic
Parfaits.*

*Nutrients per serving: Calories: 586, Total Fat: 4 g,
Protein: 1 g, Carbohydrate: 140 g, Cholesterol: 0 mg,
Sodium: 554 mg, Dietary Fiber: 1 g
Dietary Exchanges: Bread: 8*

◤UTTING CORNERS:
**To crumble cookies quickly and neatly, place
cookies in resealable plastic food storage bag. Crush
with rolling pin or meat mallet.**

EASY EASEL
RECIPES

THAI-STYLE WARM NOODLE SALAD

8 ounces uncooked angel hair pasta
½ cup chunky peanut butter
¼ cup soy sauce
¼ to ½ teaspoon red pepper flakes
2 green onions, thinly sliced
1 carrot, shredded

1. Cook pasta according to package directions.

2. While pasta is cooking, blend peanut butter, soy sauce and red pepper flakes in bowl until smooth.

3. Drain pasta, reserving 5 tablespoons water. Mix hot pasta water with peanut butter mixture until smooth; toss pasta with sauce. Stir in green onions and carrot. Serve warm or at room temperature.

Makes 4 servings

Prep and cook time: 12 minutes

Nutrients per serving: Calories: 378, Total Fat: 18 g, Protein: 16 g, Carbohydrate: 41 g, Cholesterol: 64 mg, Sodium: 1213 mg, Dietary Fiber: 4 g
Dietary Exchanges: Vegetable: 2, Bread: 2, Meat: 1, Fat: 3

Cook's Notes:

This salad is as versatile as it is easy to make. It can be prepared a day ahead and served warm or cold—perfect for potlucks, picnics and even lunch boxes. You can also make it into a heartier meal by mixing in any leftover chicken or beef.

NO-FUSS BAR COOKIES

24 graham cracker squares
1 cup (6 ounces) semisweet chocolate chips
1 cup flaked coconut
¾ cup coarsely chopped walnuts
1 can (14 ounces) sweetened condensed milk or low-fat sweetened condensed milk

1. Preheat oven to 350°F. Grease 13×9-inch baking pan; set aside. Process graham crackers in food processor until fine crumbs are formed; measure 2 cups of crumbs.

2. Combine crumbs, chips, coconut and walnuts in medium bowl; stir to blend. Add milk; stir with mixing spoon until blended. Spread batter evenly into prepared pan.

3. Bake 15 to 18 minutes or until edges are golden brown. Let pan stand on wire rack until completely cooled. Cut into 20 bars. Store bars tightly covered at room temperature or freeze up to 3 months.

Makes 20 bars

Prep and cook time: 25 minutes

Nutrients per serving: Calories: 185, Total Fat: 9 g, Protein: 4 g, Carbohydrate: 25 g, Cholesterol: 7 mg, Sodium: 77 mg, Dietary Fiber: 1 g
Dietary Exchanges: Bread: 1½, Fat: 1½

Cook's Notes:
Coconut purchased in plastic bags can be stored, unopened, at room temperature for up to 6 months. Once coconut is opened it should be stored in the refrigerator.

EASY EASEL RECIPES

BEEF & BLUE CHEESE SALAD

1 package (10 ounces) mixed green
    lettuce leaves
¼ pound sliced rare deli roast beef, cut
    into thin strips
1 large tomato, seeded and coarsely
    chopped *or* 8 large cherry tomatoes,
    halved
½ cup (2 ounces) crumbled blue or
    Gorgonzola cheese
1 cup croutons
½ cup (2 ounces) Caesar or Italian salad
    dressing

*Nutrients per serving: Calories: 269, Total Fat: 19 g,
Protein: 11 g, Carbohydrate: 12 g, Cholesterol: 33 mg,
Sodium: 528 mg, Dietary Fiber: 2 g
Dietary Exchanges: Vegetable: 1, Bread: ½, Meat: 1,
Fat: 3½*

Cook's Notes:

*Gorgonzola is one of Italy's great cheeses.
It has an ivory-colored interior that is streaked
with bluish-green veins. Gorgonzola is made from
cow's milk and has a creamy savory flavor.
This cheese can be found cut into wedges and
wrapped in foil in most supermarkets.*

1. Combine lettuce, roast
beef, tomato, cheese and
croutons in large serving
bowl.

2. Drizzle with dressing;
toss well. Serve
immediately.

       *Makes 4 main-dish or
       8 side-dish servings*

Prep time: 10 minutes

EASY EASEL RECIPES

PEANUT-MAPLE TRIANGLE PUFFS

½ **cup creamy peanut butter**

1¼ **cup powdered sugar, divided**

7 **tablespoons maple-flavored syrup, divided**

1 **package (17½ ounces) frozen puff pastry, thawed**

1. Preheat oven to 400°F. Combine peanut butter, ¼ cup powdered sugar and ¼ cup syrup in small bowl until well blended; set aside.

2. Cut each puff pastry dough sheet into 3-inch squares. Place rounded teaspoon peanut butter mixture in center of each square. Fold squares over to form triangle. Seal edges with fork.

3. Place triangles, seam-side down, about 2 inches apart onto ungreased baking sheets; spray with

cooking spray. Bake 6 to 8 minutes or until golden brown. Remove from baking sheets to wire rack to cool.

4. Combine 1 cup powdered sugar, 3 tablespoons syrup and 1 to 2 tablespoons water in small bowl. Glaze puffs just before serving.　　　　*Makes 28 puffs*

Prep and cook time: 30 minutes

Nutrients per serving (1 puff): Calories: 157, Total Fat: 9 g, Protein: 2 g, Carbohydrate: 18 g, Cholesterol: 0 mg, Sodium: 68 mg, Dietary Fiber: trace
Dietary Exchanges: Bread: 1, Fat: 2

Cook's Notes:

For longer storage, do not glaze cookies and store loosely covered so pastry dough remains crisp. Glaze before serving.

EASY EASEL RECIPES

COBB SALAD

1 package (10 ounces) torn mixed salad greens *or* 8 cups torn romaine lettuce
½ pound deli chicken, turkey or smoked turkey breast, cut ¼ inch thick
1 large tomato, seeded and chopped
⅓ cup bacon bits or crumbled crisply cooked bacon
1 large ripe avocado, peeled, seeded and diced
⅓ cup blue cheese or Caesar salad dressing

1. Place lettuce in large serving bowl.

2. Dice chicken; place in center of lettuce.

3. Arrange tomato, bacon and avocado in rows on either side of chicken.

4. Drizzle portion of dressing over salad. Serve immediately with remaining dressing.
Makes 4 main-dish or 8 side-dish servings

Prep time: 15 minutes

SERVING SUGGESTION: *Serve this colorful salad with warm French or Italian rolls.*

Nutrients per serving: Calories: 204, Total Fat: 12 g, Protein: 13 g, Carbohydrate: 11 g, Cholesterol: 28 mg, Sodium: 957 mg, Dietary Fiber: 4 g
Dietary Exchanges: Vegetable: 2, Meat: 1½, Fat: 1½

CRISPY THUMBPRINT COOKIES

1 package (18.25 ounces) yellow cake mix
½ cup vegetable oil
1 egg
3 cups crisp rice cereal, crushed
½ cup chopped walnuts
Raspberry or strawberry preserves *or* Andes mint candies, cut in half

1. Preheat oven to 375°F.

2. Combine cake mix, oil, egg and ¼ cup water. Beat at medium speed of electric mixer until well blended. Add cereal and walnuts; mix until well blended.

3. Drop by heaping teaspoonfuls about 2 inches apart onto ungreased baking sheets. Use thumb to make indentation in each cookie. Spoon about ½ teaspoon preserves into center of each cookie. (Or, place ½ of mint candy in center of each cookie.)

4. Bake 9 to 11 minutes or until golden brown. Cool cookies 1 minute on baking sheet; remove from baking sheet to wire rack to cool completely. *Makes 3 dozen cookies*

Prep and cook time: 30 minutes

Nutrients per serving (1 cookie): Calories: 136, Total Fat: 6 g, Protein: 2 g, Carbohydrate: 20 g, Cholesterol: 6 mg, Sodium: 145 mg, Dietary Fiber: trace Dietary Exchanges: Fruit: ½, Bread: 1, Fat: 1

EASY EASEL RECIPES

WARM LEMON & THYME POTATO SALAD

2 **pounds red potatoes, scrubbed and cut into ¼-inch slices**
2 **cloves garlic, minced**
¼ **cup olive oil**
2 **tablespoons bottled or fresh lemon juice**
1 **teaspoon dried thyme leaves *or*
    2 tablespoons chopped fresh thyme**
Romaine lettuce leaves

1. Bring water in large saucepan to a boil over high heat. Add potato slices. Reduce heat to medium-low. Simmer, covered, 10 minutes or until potatoes are barely tender. Pour potatoes into colander; drain well.

2. Cook garlic in oil in large deep skillet over medium heat 1 to 2 minutes. Stir in lemon juice and thyme; heat through. Add drained potatoes; stir lightly to coat potatoes with dressing. Season with salt and pepper. Reduce heat to medium-low. Cover and cook 4 to 5 minutes, turning once.

3. Arrange lettuce on 6 salad plates; top with hot potato mixture.　　*Makes 6 servings*

Prep and cook time: 30 minutes

FOR A SPECIAL TOUCH, GARNISH WITH CHERRY TOMATOES AND FRESH THYME.

Nutrients per serving:
Calories: 159, Total Fat: 1 g,
Protein: 4 g, Carbohydrate: 36 g,
Cholesterol: 0 mg,
Sodium: 12 mg,
Dietary Fiber: trace
Dietary Exchanges: Bread: 2

CHOCOLATE CHIP SHORTBREAD

½ **cup margarine or butter, softened**
½ **cup sugar**
1 **teaspoon vanilla**
1 **cup all-purpose flour**
¼ **teaspoon salt**
¼ **cup mini semisweet chocolate chips**

1. Preheat oven to 375°F. Beat margarine and sugar in large bowl until light and fluffy; beat in vanilla. Add flour and salt; beat at low speed. Stir in chips.

2. Divide dough in half. Press each half into ungreased 8-inch round cake pan.

3. Bake 12 minutes or until edges are golden brown; cut into 8 wedges per pan. Let pans stand on wire racks 10 minutes. Invert onto wire racks; cool completely. Break

into triangles. Store tightly covered at room temperature or freeze up to 3 months.

Makes 16 cookies

Prep and cook time: 30 minutes

SERVING SUGGESTION: *Serve Chocolate Chip Shortbread cookies with a tall glass of ice-cold skim milk.*

Nutrients per serving: Calories: 117, Total Fat: 6 g, Protein: 1 g, Carbohydrate: 14 g, Cholesterol: 0 mg, Sodium: 100 mg, Dietary Fiber: trace
Dietary Exchanges: Bread: 1, Fat: 1

EASY EASEL RECIPES

CHICKEN CAESAR SALAD

6 ounces chicken tenders
¼ cup plus 1 tablespoon Caesar salad dressing, divided
4 cups (about 5 ounces) prepared Italian salad mix (romaine and radicchio)
½ cup prepared croutons, divided
2 tablespoons grated Parmesan cheese

Prep and cook time: 17 minutes

Nutrients per serving: Calories: 361, Total Fat: 22 g, Protein: 24 g, Carbohydrate: 13 g, Cholesterol: 57 mg, Sodium: 244 mg, Dietary Fiber: 1 g
Dietary Exchanges: Vegetable: 1, Bread: ½, Meat: 2½, Fat: 3½

1. Cut chicken tenders in half lengthwise and crosswise. Heat 1 tablespoon salad dressing in large nonstick skillet. Add chicken; cook and stir over medium heat 3 to 4 minutes or until cooked through. Remove chicken. Sprinkle with pepper; let cool.

Serve It With Style!
To make this meal complete, just add a loaf of Italian bread or focaccia along with chocolate-dipped biscotti and fresh fruit for dessert.

2. Combine salad mix, half of croutons, remaining ¼ cup salad dressing and Parmesan in serving bowl; toss to coat. Top with remaining croutons and chicken.

Makes 2 servings

EASY EASEL RECIPES

FESTIVE FUDGE BLOSSOMS

**1 box (18.25 ounces) chocolate fudge
    cake mix**
¼ cup butter or margarine, softened
1 egg, slightly beaten
¾ to 1 cup finely chopped walnuts
48 chocolate star candies

1. Preheat oven to 350°F. Cut butter into cake mix in large bowl until mixture resembles coarse crumbs. Stir in egg and 2 tablespoons water until well blended.

2. Shape dough into ½-inch balls; roll in walnuts, pressing nuts gently into dough. Place about 2 inches apart onto ungreased baking sheets.

3. Bake cookies 12 minutes or until puffed and nearly set. Place chocolate star in center of each cookie; bake 1 minute more. Cool 2 minutes on baking sheets.

Remove cookies from baking sheets to wire rack to cool completely.

Makes 4 dozen cookies

Prep and cook time: 30 minutes

*Nutrients per serving (1 cookie): Calories: 73,
Total Fat: 4 g, Protein: 1 g, Carbohydrate: 10 g,
Cholesterol: 4 mg, Sodium: 120 mg, Dietary Fiber: trace
Dietary Exchanges: Bread: ½, Fat: 1*

· ·

Cook's Notes:

***To keep cookies fresh, store cookies in a single layer
between sheets of waxed paper.***

· ·

EASY EASEL RECIPES

ORZO AND SUMMER SQUASH SALAD

1⅓ cups (8 ounces) orzo pasta, uncooked
3 cups diced zucchini and/or yellow
    summer squash (½-inch pieces)
1 cup diced tomato
½ cup prepared light or regular Caesar
    salad dressing
1 teaspoon dried basil leaves*
Fresh spinach leaves

**¼ cup julienned basil leaves may be substituted
for dried basil leaves.*

1. Cook orzo according to package directions for 7 minutes. Add squash to orzo; return to a boil. Cook 1 to 2 minutes more or until orzo and squash are tender. Drain well; rinse under cold water to stop cooking.

2. Place mixture in large bowl; stir in tomato. Pour dressing over salad; sprinkle with basil. Toss gently to coat. Cover and refrigerate until cool. Serve salad over spinach leaves. Season to taste with salt and pepper. *Makes 6 servings, about 6 cups salad*

Prep and cook time: 25 minutes

SERVING SUGGESTION: *Serve alongside simply grilled poultry, pork or fish.*

Nutrients per serving:
Calories: 189, Total Fat: 2 g,
Protein: 7 g, Carbohydrate: 36 g,
Cholesterol: 7 mg,
Sodium: 133 mg,
Dietary Fiber: 1 g
Dietary Exchanges: Bread: 2½

EASY EASEL RECIPES

MEXICAN CHOCOLATE MACAROONS

1 package (8 ounces) semisweet baking chocolate, divided
1¾ cups plus ⅓ cup whole almonds, divided
¾ cup sugar
1 teaspoon ground cinnamon
1 teaspoon vanilla
2 egg whites

1. Preheat oven to 400°F. Grease baking sheets; set aside.

2. Place 5 squares of chocolate in food processor; process until coarsely chopped. Add 1¾ cups almonds and sugar; process using on/off pulsing action until mixture is finely ground. Add cinnamon, vanilla and egg whites; process just until mixture forms moist dough.

3. Form dough into 1-inch balls (dough will be sticky). Place about 2 inches apart onto prepared baking sheets. Press 1 almond on top of each cookie.

4. Bake 8 to 10 minutes or just until set. Cool 2 minutes on baking sheets. Remove cookies from baking sheets to wire rack to cool.

5. Heat remaining 3 squares chocolate in saucepan over very low heat until melted. Drizzle chocolate over cookies.

Makes 3 dozen cookies

Prep and cook time:
30 minutes

Nutrients per serving (1 cookie):
Calories: 87, Total Fat: 5 g,
Protein: 2 g, Carbohydrate: 9 g,
Cholesterol: 0 mg, Sodium: 4 mg,
Dietary Fiber: 1 g
Dietary Exchanges: Bread: ½,
Fat: 1

EASY EASEL RECIPES

PEAR AND CRANBERRY SALAD

½ **cup canned whole-berry cranberry sauce**

2 **tablespoons balsamic vinegar**

1 **tablespoon olive or canola oil**

12 **cups (9 ounces) packed assorted bitter or gourmet salad greens**

6 **small *or* 4 large pears (about 1¾ pounds)**

½ **cup (2 ounces) crumbled blue or Gorgonzola cheese**

1. Combine cranberry sauce, vinegar and oil in small bowl; mix well. (Dressing may be covered and refrigerated up to 2 days before serving.)

2. Arrange greens on 6 serving plates. Cut pears lengthwise into ½-inch-thick slices; cut core and seeds from each slice. Arrange pears attractively over greens. Drizzle cranberry dressing over pears and greens; sprinkle with cheese. Season with pepper. *Makes 6 servings*

Prep time: 20 minutes

Nutrients per serving: Calories: 61, Total Fat: 6 g, Protein: 4 g, Carbohydrate: 26 g, Cholesterol: 7 mg, Sodium: 165 mg, Dietary Fiber: 2 g
Dietary Exchanges: Fruit: 2, Fat: 1

Cook's Notes:
Be sure to use ripe pears. Forelles and Red Bartletts are particularly well suited for use in this salad.

EASY EASEL RECIPES

CHOCOLATE MINT RAVIOLI COOKIES

1 package (15 ounces) refrigerated pie crusts
1 bar (7 ounces) cookies 'n' mint chocolate candy
1 egg
   Powdered sugar

1. Preheat oven to 400°F. Unfold 1 pie crust on lightly floured surface. Roll into 13-inch circle. Using 2½-inch cutters, cut pastry into 24 (2½-inch) circles with cookie cutters, rerolling scraps if necessary. Repeat with remaining pie crust.

2. Separate candy bar into pieces marked in chocolate. Cut each chocolate piece in half. Beat egg and 1 tablespoon water together in small bowl with fork. Brush half of pastry circles lightly with egg mixture. Place 1 piece of chocolate in center of circles (there will be some candy bar left over). Top with remaining pastry circles. Seal edges with tines of fork.

3. Place on ungreased baking sheets. Brush with egg mixture.

4. Bake cookies 8 to 10 minutes or until golden brown. Remove from cookie sheets; cool completely on wire rack. Dust with powdered sugar.   ***Makes 2 dozen cookies***

Prep and cook time: 30 minutes

Nutrients per serving:
Calories: 118, Total Fat: 6 g,
Protein: 2 g, Carbohydrate: 14 g,
Cholesterol: 14 mg,
Sodium: 96 mg, Dietary Fiber: 0 g
Dietary Exchanges: Fruit: ½,
Bread: ½, Fat: 1

PESTO & TORTELLINI SOUP

1 package (9 ounces) fresh cheese tortellini

3 cans (about 14 ounces each) chicken broth

1 jar (7 ounces) roasted red peppers, drained and slivered

¾ cup frozen green peas

3 to 4 cups fresh spinach, washed and stems removed

1 to 2 tablespoons pesto _or_ ¼ cup grated Parmesan cheese

1. Cook tortellini according to package directions; drain.

2. While pasta is cooking, bring broth to a boil over high heat in covered Dutch oven. Add cooked tortellini, peppers and peas; return to a boil. Reduce heat to medium; simmer 1 minute.

3. Remove soup from heat; stir in spinach and pesto.　　　　　*Makes 6 servings*

Prep and cook time: 14 minutes

*Nutrients per serving: Calories: 144, Total Fat: 4 g,
Protein: 10 g, Carbohydrate: 18 g, Cholesterol: 9 mg,
Sodium: 754 mg, Dietary Fiber: 2 g
Dietary Exchanges: Bread: 1, Meat: ½, Fat: 1*

Cook's Notes:

*A Dutch oven is a large pot or kettle with
a tight-fitting lid that prevents the steam
from escaping while cooking.*

CASHEW–LEMON SHORTBREAD COOKIES

- ½ **cup roasted cashews**
- 1 **cup butter or margarine, softened**
- ½ **cup sugar**
- 2 **teaspoons lemon extract**
- 1 **teaspoon vanilla**
- 2 **cups all-purpose flour**

1. Preheat oven to 325°F. Place cashews in food processor; process until finely ground. Add butter, sugar, lemon extract and vanilla; process until well blended. Add flour; process using on/off pulsing action until dough is well blended and begins to form ball.

2. Shape dough into 1½-inch balls; roll in additional sugar. Place about 2 inches apart onto ungreased baking sheets; flatten with bottom of glass.

3. Bake cookies 17 to 19 minutes or just until set and edges are lightly browned. Remove cookies from baking sheets to wire rack to cool.   *Makes 2 to 2½ dozen cookies*

Prep and cook time: 30 minutes

Nutrients per serving (1 cookie): Calories: 140, Total Fat: 9 g, Protein: 2 g, Carbohydrate: 13 g, Cholesterol: 0 mg, Sodium: 89 mg, Dietary Fiber: trace Dietary Exchanges: Bread: 1, Fat: 1½

EASY EASEL RECIPES

POTATO-BACON SOUP

2 cans (about 14 ounces each) chicken broth
3 russet potatoes (1¾ to 2 pounds), peeled and cut into ½-inch cubes
1 medium onion, finely chopped
1 teaspoon dried thyme leaves
4 to 6 strips bacon (4 to 6 ounces), chopped
½ cup (2 ounces) shredded Cheddar cheese

1. Combine broth, potatoes, onion and thyme in Dutch oven; bring to a boil over high heat. Reduce heat to medium-high and boil 10 minutes or until potatoes are tender.

2. While potatoes are cooking, place bacon in microwavable container. Cover with paper towels and cook on HIGH 6 to 7 minutes or until bacon is crisp, stirring after 3 minutes. Break up bacon.

3. Immediately transfer bacon to broth mixture with slotted spoon; simmer 3 to 5 minutes. Season to taste with salt and pepper. Ladle into bowls and sprinkle with cheese. *Makes 4 servings*

Prep and cook time: 27 minutes

Nutrients per serving: Calories: 406, Total Fat: 19 g, Protein: 18 g, Carbohydrate: 43 g, Cholesterol: 48 mg, Sodium: 1451 mg, Dietary Fiber: 1 g Dietary Exchanges: Bread: 3, Meat: 1, Fat: 3

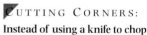

CUTTING **C**ORNERS:
Instead of using a knife to chop the bacon, try snipping it with a pair of scissors while it is partially frozen—you'll find this method quicker and easier.

EASY EASEL RECIPES

Fuss-Free Sweets

Raspberry Napoleons (page 120)

STIR-FRY BEEF & VEGETABLE SOUP

- **1 pound boneless beef steak, such as sirloin or round steak**
- **2 teaspoons Oriental sesame oil, divided**
- **3 cans (about 14 ounces each) reduced-sodium beef broth**
- **1 package (16 ounces) frozen stir-fry vegetables**
- **3 green onions, thinly sliced**
- **¼ cup stir-fry sauce**

1. Slice beef across grain into ⅛-inch-thick strips; cut strips into bite-size pieces.

2. Heat Dutch oven over high heat. Add 1 teaspoon oil and tilt pan to coat bottom. Add half the beef in single layer; cook 1 minute, without stirring, until slightly browned on bottom. Turn and brown other side

1 minute. Remove beef from pan with slotted spoon; set aside. Repeat with remaining 1 teaspoon oil and beef; set aside.

3. Add broth to Dutch oven; cover and bring to a boil over high heat. Add vegetables; reduce heat to medium-high and simmer 3 to 5 minutes or until heated through. Add beef, green onions and stir-fry sauce; simmer 1 minute more. *Makes 6 servings*

Prep and cook time: 22 minutes

Nutrients per serving:
Calories: 159, Total Fat: 5 g,
Protein: 20 g, Carbohydrate: 7 g,
Cholesterol: 43 mg,
Sodium: 356 mg,
Dietary Fiber: trace
Dietary Exchanges: Bread: ½,
Meat: 2

RICE PILAF WITH DRIED CHERRIES AND ALMONDS

½ **cup slivered almonds**
2 **tablespoons margarine or butter**
2 **cups converted rice**
½ **cup chopped onion**
1 **can (14½ ounces) vegetable broth**
½ **cup dried cherries**

1. To toast almonds, cook and stir in large skillet over medium heat until lightly browned. Remove from skillet; cool.

2. Melt margarine in large skillet over low heat. Add rice and onion. Cook and stir until rice is lightly browned. Add broth and 1½ cups water. Bring to a boil over high heat. Reduce heat to low. Simmer, covered, 15 minutes.

3. Stir in almonds and cherries. Simmer 5 minutes or until liquid is absorbed and rice is tender. *Makes 12 servings*

FOR A SPECIAL TOUCH, GARNISH WITH FRESH ITALIAN PARSLEY.

Nutrients per serving: Calories: 174, Total Fat: 5 g, Protein: 3 g, Carbohydrate: 29 g, Cholesterol: 0 mg, Sodium: 37 mg, Dietary Fiber: 1 g
Dietary Exchanges: Bread: 2, Fat: 1

Cook's Notes:
A pilaf is a rice (or bulgur) dish which originated in the Near East. It was prepared by browning rice in fat before cooking it in broth. This process lends a slightly nutty flavor and helps to keep the grains separate.

EASY EASEL RECIPES

MINESTRONE SOUP

¾ **cup small shell pasta**

2 **cans (about 14 ounces each) vegetable broth**

1 **can (28 ounces) crushed tomatoes in tomato purée**

1 **can (15 ounces) white beans, drained and rinsed**

1 **package (16 ounces) frozen vegetable medley, such as broccoli, green beans, carrots and red peppers**

4 **to 6 teaspoons prepared pesto**

1. Bring 4 cups water to a boil in large saucepan over high heat. Stir in pasta; cook 8 to 10 minutes or until tender. Drain.

2. While pasta is cooking, combine broth, tomatoes and beans in Dutch oven. Cover and bring to a boil over high heat. Reduce heat to low; simmer 3 to 5 minutes.

3. Add vegetables to broth mixture and return to a boil over high heat. Stir in pasta. Ladle soup into bowls; spoon about 1 teaspoon pesto in center of each serving.

Makes 4 to 6 servings

Prep and cook time: 20 minutes

Nutrients per serving: Calories: 359, Total Fat: 5 g, Protein: 18 g, Carbohydrate: 71 g, Cholesterol: 1 mg, Sodium: 904 mg, Dietary Fiber: 14 g
Dietary Exchanges: Vegetable: 1, Bread: 4, Fat: 1

EASY EASEL RECIPES

BROILED ZUCCHINI HALVES

½ **cup (2 ounces) shredded mozzarella cheese**
2 **tablespoons diced pimiento**
2 **tablespoons chopped ripe olives**
4 **small zucchini (about 1 pound total), sliced lengthwise**
1 **tablespoon olive oil**

1. Preheat broiler; place oven rack 6 inches below heat source. Combine cheese, pimiento and olives in small bowl; set aside.

2. Brush both sides of zucchini halves with oil; arrange on boiler pan lined with foil. Broil 5 minutes or until fork-tender.

3. Spoon about 2 tablespoons cheese mixture along each zucchini half. Broil until cheese melts and browns. Serve immediately.
    Makes 4 side-dish servings

Prep and cook time: 15 minutes

FOR A SPECIAL TOUCH, GARNISH WITH TARRAGON LEAVES.

Nutrients per serving: Calories: 95, Total Fat: 7 g, Protein: 4 g, Carbohydrate: 4 g, Cholesterol: 11 mg, Sodium: 168 mg, Dietary Fiber: 1 g
Dietary Exchanges: Vegetable: 1, Fat: 1½

Cook's Notes:

Small zucchini are younger, more tender and have thinner skins than larger zucchini. When purchasing, look for glossy, dark green skins.

EASY EASEL RECIPES

Extra Easy Meats

Pepper Steak (page 27)

FRENCHED BEANS WITH CELERY

½ teaspoon vegetable oil

2 tablespoons sunflower seeds

¾ pound fresh green beans, sliced
    lengthwise

2 ribs celery, sliced thin on diagonal

2 tablespoons margarine or butter,
    melted

1. To toast sunflower seeds, heat ½ teaspoon oil in small skillet over medium heat. Add sunflower seeds. Cook and stir until lightly browned. Remove from skillet; cool.

2. Bring ¼ cup water in 2-quart saucepan to a boil over high heat. Add beans and celery. Reduce heat to medium-low. Simmer, covered, 8 minutes or until beans are crisp-tender; drain.

3. Toss beans and celery with margarine. Place in serving dish and sprinkle with sunflower seeds. Serve immediately.

Makes 6 side-dish servings

Prep and cook time: 20 minutes

FOR A SPECIAL TOUCH, GARNISH WITH CELERY LEAVES AND CARROT SLICES.

Nutrients per serving: Calories: 70, Total Fat: 6 g, Protein: 2 g, Carbohydrate: 4 g, Cholesterol: 0 mg, Sodium: 62 mg, Dietary Fiber: trace
Dietary Exchanges: Vegetable: 1, Fat: 1

PEPPER STEAK

1 tablespoon coarsely cracked black pepper
½ teaspoon dried rosemary
2 beef filets mignons or rib-eye steaks, 1 inch thick (4 to 6 ounces each)
1 tablespoon butter or margarine
1 tablespoon vegetable oil
¼ cup brandy or dry red wine

1. Combine pepper and rosemary in bowl. Coat both sides of steaks with mixture.

2. Heat butter and oil in large skillet until hot; add steaks and cook over medium to medium-high heat 5 to 7 minutes per side for medium, or to desired degree of doneness. Remove steaks from skillet. Sprinkle lightly with salt and cover to keep warm.

3. Add brandy to skillet; bring to a boil over high heat, scraping particles from bottom of skillet. Boil about 1 minute or until liquid is reduced by half. Spoon sauce over steaks.

Makes 2 servings

Prep and cook time: 17 minutes

FOR A SPECIAL TOUCH, SPRINKLE CHOPPED PARSLEY OVER STEAKS BEFORE SERVING.

Nutrients per serving: Calories: 392, Total Fat: 24 g, Protein: 25 g, Carbohydrate: 2 g, Cholesterol: 84 mg, Sodium: 117 mg, Dietary Fiber: 1 g
Dietary Exchanges: Meat: 3½, Fat: 2½

Cook's Notes:

Filets mignons and rib-eye steaks are tender cuts of meat. These choice cuts are the most expensive and well-suited to quick, dry-heat cooking methods, such as pan-frying, roasting, broiling and grilling.

EASY EASEL RECIPES

PEAS WITH CUKES 'N' DILL

½ **medium cucumber, peeled and seeded**
2 **tablespoons margarine or butter**
2 **pounds fresh peas, shelled *or***
   **1 package (10 ounce) frozen peas,
     thawed**
1 **teaspoon dried dill weed**

1. Cut cucumber into ¼-inch slices. Heat margarine in medium skillet over medium-high heat until melted and bubbly. Add peas and cucumber. Cook and stir 5 minutes until vegetables are crisp-tender.

2. Stir in dill weed and season to taste with salt and pepper. Place in serving dish. Serve immediately.

Makes 4 side-dish servings

Prep and cook time:
25 minutes

***FOR A SPECIAL TOUCH,
GARNISH WITH FRESH DILL.***

Nutrients per serving: Calories: 237, Total Fat: 6 g, Protein: 12 g, Carbohydrate: 35 g, Cholesterol: 0 mg, Sodium: 73 mg, Dietary Fiber: 0 g Dietary Exchanges: Bread: 2½, Fat: 1

Cook's Notes:

As cucumbers mature, the seeds grow larger and more bitter. To seed a cucumber, cut it in half lengthwise and use a teaspoon to scrape out the seeds.

EASY EASEL RECIPES

BEEF TERIYAKI STIR-FRY

1 cup uncooked rice
1 pound beef sirloin, thinly sliced
½ cup teriyaki marinade, divided
2 tablespoons vegetable oil, divided
1 medium onion, halved and sliced
2 cups frozen green beans, rinsed and
    drained

1. Cook rice according to package directions, omitting salt.

2. Combine beef and ¼ cup marinade in medium bowl; set aside.

3. Heat ½ tablespoon oil in wok or large skillet over medium-high heat until hot. Add onion; stir-fry 3 to 4 minutes or until crisp-tender. Remove from wok to medium bowl.

4. Heat ½ tablespoon oil in wok until hot. Stir-fry

beans 3 minutes or until crisp-tender and hot. Drain off excess liquid. Add beans to onion in bowl.

5. Heat remaining 1 tablespoon oil in wok until hot. Drain beef, discarding marinade. Stir-fry beef about 3 minutes or until browned. Stir in vegetables and remaining ¼ cup marinade; cook and stir 1 minute or until heated through. Serve with rice.

Makes 4 servings

Prep and cook time: 22 minutes

Nutrients per serving:
Calories: 407, Total Fat: 12 g,
Protein: 27 g, Carbohydrate: 46 g,
Cholesterol: 65 mg,
Sodium: 396 mg,
Dietary Fiber: 1 g
Dietary Exchanges: Vegetable: 3,
Bread: 2, Meat: 2½, Fat: 1

EASY EASEL RECIPES

CARROT AND PARSNIP PURÉE

1 **pound carrots, peeled and cut crosswise into ½-inch pieces**
1 **pound parsnips, peeled and cut crosswise into ½-inch pieces**
1 **cup chopped onion**
1 **cup clear vegetable broth**
1 **tablespoon margarine or butter**
⅛ **teaspoon ground nutmeg**

Prep and cook time: 30 minutes

Nutrients per serving: Calories: 78, Total Fat: 1 g, Protein: 1 g, Carbohydrate: 16 g, Cholesterol: 0 mg, Sodium: 56 mg, Dietary Fiber: 3 g Dietary Exchanges: Vegetable: 3

Cook's Notes:

If you want to prepare this dish ahead of time, transfer the completed purée to a microwavable casserole and chill up to 24 hours. To reheat, microwave covered at HIGH 6 to 7 minutes or until hot, stirring after 4 minutes of cooking.

1. Combine carrots, parsnips, onion and vegetable broth in medium saucepan. Cover; bring to a boil over high heat. Reduce heat to low. Simmer, covered, 20 minutes or until vegetables are very tender.

2. Drain vegetables, reserving broth. Combine vegetables, margarine, nutmeg and ¼ cup broth in food processor. Process until smooth. Serve immediately.

Makes 10 servings

SKEWERED BEEF STRIPS WITH SPICY HONEY GLAZE

1 pound beef top sirloin steak
⅓ cup soy sauce
2 tablespoons white vinegar
1 teaspoon ground ginger
⅛ teaspoon ground red pepper
⅓ cup honey

1. Slice beef across grain into ¼-inch-thick strips. Thread beef strips onto 12 wooden skewers and place in large glass baking dish. (Soak skewers in cold water 20 minutes before using to prevent them from burning.)

2. Heat broiler or prepare grill. Combine soy sauce, vinegar, ginger and ground red pepper; pour over skewers and marinate 10 minutes, turning once.

3. Drain marinade into small saucepan; stir in honey and brush mixture over beef. Bring remaining mixture to a boil; boil 2 minutes.

4. Broil or grill skewered beef 3 to 4 minutes. Serve remaining honey glaze as dipping sauce.   ***Makes 4 servings***

Prep and cook time: 30 minutes

SERVING SUGGESTION: ***Serve skewers over rice; drizzle rice with remaining honey glaze.***

Nutrients per serving:
Calories: 241, Total Fat: 5 g,
Protein: 24 g, Carbohydrate: 25 g,
Cholesterol: 65 mg,
Sodium: 1420 mg,
Dietary Fiber: trace
Dietary Exchanges: Fruit: 1½,
Meat: 3

JAMAICAN GRILLED SWEET POTATOES

2 large (about 1½ pounds) sweet
    potatoes or yams
3 tablespoons packed brown sugar
2 tablespoons margarine or butter,
    softened, divided
1 teaspoon ground ginger
2 teaspoons dark rum
1 tablespoon chopped fresh cilantro

1. Pierce potatoes with fork; place on paper towel in microwave. Microwave at HIGH 5 to 6 minutes or until slightly undercooked, rotating ¼ turn halfway through cooking. Let stand 10 minutes. Diagonally slice about ½ inch off ends of potatoes; continue cutting potatoes diagonally into ¾-inch-thick slices.

2. Combine brown sugar, 1 tablespoon margarine and ginger in small bowl; mix well. Stir in rum, then cilantro; set aside.

3. Melt remaining 1 tablespoon margarine. With half of melted margarine, lightly brush one side of each potato slice. Place slices margarine-side down on grid over medium coals. Grill over covered grill 4 to 6 minutes or until grillmarked. Brush tops with remaining melted margarine; turn over and grill 3 to 5 minutes or until grillmarked. To serve, spoon rum mixture over potato slices.

Makes 6 servings

Prep and cook time: 30 minutes

Nutrients per serving: Calories: 195, Total Fat: 4 g, Protein: 2 g, Carbohydrate: 38 g, Cholesterol: 0 mg, Sodium: 56 mg, Dietary Fiber: 0 g
Dietary Exchanges: Bread: 2½, Fat: ½

BEEF STROGANOFF

12 ounces wide egg noodles
1 can (10¾ ounces) condensed cream of mushroom soup
1 cup (8 ounces) sour cream
1 packet (1¼ ounces) dry onion soup mix
1¼ to 1½ pounds lean ground beef
½ (10-ounce) package frozen peas

1. Place 3 quarts water in 8-quart stock pot; bring to a boil over high heat. Stir in noodles; boil, uncovered, 6 minutes or until tender. Drain.

2. Meanwhile, place mushroom soup, sour cream and onion soup mix in medium bowl. Stir until blended; set aside. Place meat in large skillet; cook over high heat 6 to 8 minutes or until meat is no longer pink, breaking meat apart with wooden

spoon. Pour off drippings. Reduce heat to low. Add soup mixture; stir over low heat until bubbly. Stir in peas; heat through. Serve over noodles. *Makes 6 servings*

Prep and cook time: 20 minutes

Nutrients per serving: Calories: 545, Total Fat: 26 g, Protein: 28 g, Carbohydrate: 48 g, Cholesterol: 148 mg, Sodium: 1011 mg, Dietary Fiber: trace Dietary Exchanges: Bread: 3, Meat: 2½, Fat: 4

Serve It With Style!
To make this meal complete, simply add fresh fruit and a tossed green salad.

EASY EASEL RECIPES

CHUTNEY'D SQUASH CIRCLES

2 acorn squash (1 pound each)
2 tablespoons margarine or butter
½ cup prepared chutney

1. Preheat oven to 400°F. Cut squash crosswise into ¾-inch circles; scoop out seeds.

2. Place foil in 13×9-inch baking dish; dot foil with margarine. Place squash on margarine; slightly overlap. Spoon chutney over slices and sprinkle with 2 tablespoons water. Fold foil toward the center crimping ends to form tight seal.

3. Bake 20 to 30 minutes until tender. Place on serving plate; pour drippings over squash. Serve immediately.

Makes 4 side-dish servings

Prep and cook time:
35 minutes

Nutrients per serving: Calories: 204, Total Fat: 7 g, Protein: 2 g, Carbohydrate: 37 g, Cholesterol: 0 mg, Sodium: 76 mg, Dietary Fiber: 1 g
Dietary Exchanges: Bread: 2, Fat: 1

Cook's Notes:

Chutney is a spicy relish made with fruit, vinegar, sugar and spices. Chutney can be chunky or smooth in texture. It's a great accompaniment that adds flavor to dishes.

EASY EASEL RECIPES

CHILI-STUFFED POBLANO PEPPERS

1 pound lean ground beef
4 large poblano peppers
1 can (15 ounces) chili-seasoned beans
1 can (14½ ounces) chili-style chunky tomatoes, undrained
1 tablespoon Mexican (Adobo) seasoning
⅔ cup (about 2½ ounces) shredded Mexican cheese blend or Monterey Jack cheese

1. Preheat broiler. Cook ground beef in large nonstick skillet over medium-high heat 5 to 6 minutes or until no longer pink.

2. Meanwhile, bring 2 quarts water to a boil in 3-quart saucepan. Cut peppers in half lengthwise; remove stems and seeds. Add 4 pepper halves to boiling water; cook 3 minutes or until bright green and slightly softened. Remove; drain upside down on plate. Repeat with remaining 4 halves. Set aside.

3. Add beans, tomatoes and Mexican seasoning to ground beef. Cook and stir over medium heat 5 minutes or until mixture thickens slightly.

4. Arrange peppers, cut sides up, in 13×9-inch baking dish. Divide chili mixture evenly among peppers; top with cheese. Broil 6 inches from heat 1 minute or until cheese is melted. Serve immediately.

Makes 4 servings

Prep and cook time: 26 minutes

SERVING SUGGESTION: *Serve stuffed peppers with corn bread and chunky salsa.*

Nutrients per serving: Calories: 546, Total Fat: 22 g, Protein: 40 g, Carbohydrate: 47 g, Cholesterol: 87 mg, Sodium: 1448 mg, Dietary Fiber: 2 g
Dietary Exchanges: Vegetable: 3, Bread: 2, Meat: 3½, Fat: 2½

HAM AND CHEESE CORN MUFFINS

1 package (8½ ounces) corn muffin mix
½ cup chopped deli ham
½ cup (2 ounces) shredded Swiss cheese
⅓ cup 2% milk
1 egg
1 tablespoon Dijon mustard

1. Preheat oven to 400°F. Combine muffin mix, ham and cheese in medium bowl.

2. Combine milk, egg and mustard in 1-cup glass measure. Stir milk mixture into dry ingredients; mix just until moistened.

3. Coat 9 (2¾-inch) muffin cups with nonstick cooking spray. Fill cups two-thirds full with batter.

4. Bake 18 to 20 minutes or until light golden brown. Remove muffin pan to

cooling rack. Let stand 5 minutes. Serve warm.   *Makes 9 muffins*

Prep and cook time: 30 minutes

Nutrients per serving (1 muffin): Calories: 152, Total Fat: 5 g, Protein: 7 g, Carbohydrate: 21 g, Cholesterol: 34 mg, Sodium: 409 mg, Dietary Fiber: trace Dietary Exchanges: Bread: 1, Meat: ½, Fat: ½

Serve It With Style!

For added flavor, serve Ham and Cheese Corn Muffins with honey-flavored butter. To prepare, stir together equal amounts of honey and softened butter.

SWEET AND SOUR BEEF

1 pound lean ground beef

1 small onion, thinly sliced

2 teaspoons minced fresh ginger

1 package (16 ounces) frozen mixed vegetables (snap peas, carrots, water chestnuts, pineapple and red pepper)

6 to 8 tablespoons bottled sweet and sour sauce or sauce from frozen mixed vegetables

Cooked rice

Prep and cook time: 15 minutes

SERVING SUGGESTION: *Serve Sweet and Sour Beef with sliced Asian apple-pears.*

Nutrients per serving: Calories: 292, Total Fat: 15 g, Protein: 21 g, Carbohydrate: 19 g, Cholesterol: 70 mg, Sodium: 182 mg, Dietary Fiber: 3 g
Dietary Exchanges: Vegetable: 2, Bread: 1/2, Meat: 3, Fat: 1

Cook's Notes:

To mince ginger, peel it with a vegetable peeler and chop it with a paring knife until the ginger is in uniform fine pieces.

1. Place meat, onion and ginger in large skillet; cook over high heat 6 to 8 minutes or until no longer pink, breaking apart with spoon. Pour off drippings.

2. Stir in frozen vegetables and sauce. Cook, covered, 6 to 8 minutes, stirring every 2 minutes or until vegetables are heated through. Serve over rice.

Makes 4 servings

EASY EASEL RECIPES

Fast-Fixin' Sides

Broiled Zucchini Halves (page 104)

ALL-IN-ONE BURGER STEW

1 **pound lean ground beef**
2 **cups frozen Italian vegetables**
1 **can (14½ ounces) chopped tomatoes with basil and garlic**
1 **can (about 14 ounces) beef broth**
2½ **cups uncooked medium egg noodles**

1. Cook meat in Dutch oven or skillet over medium-high heat until no longer pink; break meat apart with wooden spoon. Drain.

2. Add vegetables, tomatoes and broth; bring to a boil over high heat.

3. Add noodles; reduce heat to medium. Cover and cook 12 to 15 minutes or until noodles have absorbed liquid and vegetables are tender. Add salt and pepper to taste.

Makes 6 servings

Prep and cook time: 25 minutes

FOR A SPECIAL TOUCH, SPRINKLE WITH CHOPPED PARSLEY BEFORE SERVING.

Nutrients per serving: Calories: 245, Total Fat: 11 g, Protein: 18 g, Carbohydrate: 18 g, Cholesterol: 62 mg, Sodium: 458 mg, Dietary Fiber: 2 g
Dietary Exchanges: Vegetable: 1, Bread: 1, Meat: 2, Fat: 1

Serve It With Style!

To complete this meal, serve with breadsticks or a loaf of Italian bread and a mixed green and tomato salad.

EASY EASEL RECIPES

GREEK ISLES OMELET

¼ **cup chopped onion**

¼ **cup chopped, rinsed canned artichoke hearts**

¼ **cup chopped, washed and torn spinach leaves**

¼ **cup chopped plum tomato**

1 **cup cholesterol-free egg substitute**

2 **tablespoons sliced pitted ripe olives, drained and rinsed**

1. Spray small nonstick skillet with cooking spray; heat over medium heat until hot. Cook and stir onion 2 minutes or until crisp-tender.

2. Add artichoke hearts. Cook and stir until heated through. Add spinach and tomato; toss briefly. Remove from heat. Transfer vegetables to small bowl. Wipe out skillet and spray with nonstick cooking spray.

3. Combine egg substitute and olives in medium bowl. Season with pepper. Heat skillet over medium heat until hot. Pour egg mixture into skillet. Cook over medium heat 5 to 7 minutes. As eggs begin to set, gently lift edges of omelet with spatula and tilt skillet so that uncooked portion flows underneath.

4. When egg mixture is set, spoon vegetable mixture over half of omelet. Loosen omelet with spatula and fold in half. Slide omelet onto serving plate.

Makes 2 servings

Prep and cook time:
20 minutes

Nutrients per serving:
Calories: 106, Total Fat: 3 g,
Protein: 12 g, Carbohydrate: 8 g,
Cholesterol: 0 mg,
Sodium: 512 mg,
Dietary Fiber: 2 g
Dietary Exchanges:
Vegetable: 1½, Meat: 1½

PORK MEDALLIONS WITH MARSALA

**1 pound pork tenderloin, cut into
 ½-inch-thick slices**
All-purpose flour
2 tablespoons olive oil
1 clove garlic, minced
½ cup sweet Marsala wine
2 tablespoons chopped fresh parsley

1. Lightly dust pork with flour. Heat oil in large skillet over medium-high heat until hot. Add pork slices; cook 3 minutes per side or until browned. Remove from pan. Reduce heat to medium.

2. Add garlic to skillet; cook and stir 1 minute. Add pork and wine; cook 3 minutes or until pork is barely pink in center. Remove pork from skillet.

Stir in parsley. Simmer wine mixture until slightly thickened, 2 to 3 minutes. Serve over pork. *Makes 4 servings*

Prep and cook time: 20 minutes

FOR A SPECIAL TOUCH, SPRINKLE WITH CHOPPED RED ONION JUST BEFORE SERVING.

Nutrients per serving: Calories: 218, Total Fat: 11 g, Protein: 24 g, Carbohydrate: 1 g, Cholesterol: 65 mg, Sodium: 67 mg, Dietary Fiber: trace Dietary Exchanges: Meat: 3, Fat: 1

Cook's Notes:
Marsala is a rich smoky-flavored wine imported from the Mediterranean island of Sicily. This sweet varietal is served with dessert or used for cooking. Dry Marsala is served as a before-dinner drink.

EASY EASEL RECIPES

TORTELLINI WITH ARTICHOKES, OLIVES AND FETA CHEESE

2 packages (9 ounces) refrigerated cheese-filled spinach tortellini
2 jars (4 ounces) marinated artichoke heart quarters, drained*
2 medium carrots, sliced diagonally
½ cup sliced pitted ripe olives
½ cup (2 ounces) crumbled feta cheese
½ cup cheese-garlic Italian salad dressing

*For additional flavor, add artichoke marinade to tortellini along with salad dressing.

1. Cook tortellini according to package directions. Remove and rinse well under cold water until pasta is cool.

2. Combine tortellini, artichoke hearts, carrots, olives and feta cheese in large bowl. Add salad dressing, tossing lightly to coat. Season to taste with pepper.

Makes 6 servings

Prep and cook time: 23 minutes

SERVING SUGGESTION: *Serve with whole wheat dinner rolls and wedges of fresh melon such as honeydew, watermelon and cantaloupe.*

Nutrients per serving:
Calories: 319, Total Fat: 19 g,
Protein: 9 g, Carbohydrate: 31 g,
Cholesterol: 23 mg,
Sodium: 824 mg,
Dietary Fiber: 3 g
Dietary Exchanges: Vegetable: 1,
Bread: 2, Fat: 3

PORK SCHNITZEL

**4 boneless pork chops, ¼ inch thick
(3 ounces each)**
**½ cup corn flake crumbs or cracker
crumbs**
1 egg, lightly beaten
2 to 4 teaspoons olive oil, divided
⅓ cup lemon juice
¼ cup chicken broth

1. Preheat oven to 200°F. Place ovenproof platter or baking sheet in oven. Trim fat from pork chops; discard. Place pork chops between layers of waxed paper; pound with smooth side of mallet to ⅛ to ¼ inch thick. Place crumbs in medium bowl. Dip 1 pork chop at a time in egg; gently shake off excess. Dip in crumbs to coat both sides. Place breaded pork chops in single layer on plate. Sprinkle with pepper.

2. Heat 2 teaspoons oil in large skillet over medium-high heat until hot. Add pork chops in single layer. Cook 1 minute or until golden brown on bottoms. Turn and cook ½ to 1 minute or until golden brown and pork is no longer pink in center. Transfer to platter in oven. Repeat to cook remaining pork chops, adding oil as needed to prevent meat from sticking to pan. Transfer to platter in oven.

3. Remove skillet from heat. Add lemon juice and broth. Stir to scrape cooked bits from pan bottom. Return to heat; bring to a boil, stirring constantly, until liquid is reduced to 3 to 4 tablespoons. Remove platter from oven. Pour liquid over meat.

Makes 4 servings

Prep and cook time: 20 minutes

Nutrients per serving: Calories: 245, Total Fat: 12 g, Protein: 21 g, Carbohydrate: 13 g, Cholesterol: 95 mg, Sodium: 273 mg, Dietary Fiber: 1 g
Dietary Exchanges: Bread: 1, Meat: 3, Fat: ½

EASY EASEL RECIPES

LINGUINE WITH ASPARAGUS AND ASIAGO

1 pound fresh asparagus, cut into 1-inch pieces
16 ounces uncooked linguine, broken in half
1 tablespoon butter or margarine
1 cup (4 ounces) shredded Asiago or grated Parmesan cheese
½ cup sour cream
½ cup pitted ripe olive slices

1. Place 3 quarts of water in Dutch oven; cover and bring to a boil over high heat.

2. Drop asparagus into boiling water; boil 1 to 2 minutes or until crisp-tender. Remove with slotted spoon; rinse under cold water. Drain.

3. Add linguine to boiling water; cook according to package directions until *al dente*. Drain.

4. Combine linguine and butter in large bowl; toss gently until butter is melted. Add asparagus, cheese, sour cream and olives; toss gently until linguine is coated and cheese is melted. Season to taste with salt and pepper. Serve immediately.

Makes 4 servings

Prep and cook time:
30 minutes

Nutrients per serving:
Calories: 717, Total Fat: 27 g,
Protein: 26 g, Carbohydrate: 96 g,
Cholesterol: 46 mg,
Sodium: 1023 mg,
Dietary Fiber: 0 g
Dietary Exchanges: Vegetable: 1,
Bread: 6, Meat: 1, Fat: 4½

EASY EASEL RECIPES

MAPLE-CRANBERRY PORK CHOPS

4 well-trimmed center cut pork chops
(½ inch thick)
1 cup dry red wine or apple juice
½ cup maple syrup*
½ cup dried cranberries
2 teaspoons cornstarch

*Pure maple or maple-flavored syrup may be used.

1. Spray large nonstick skillet with nonstick cooking spray. Heat skillet over medium-high heat until hot. Add pork chops; cook 3 to 5 minutes per side or just until browned and pork is no longer pink in center. Remove from skillet; keep warm.

2. Add wine, syrup and cranberries to skillet; cook and stir over medium-high heat 2 to 3 minutes.

3. Combine 1 tablespoon water and cornstarch in small bowl; stir until smooth. Add cornstarch mixture to skillet; cook and stir about 1 minute or until thickened and clear. Reduce heat to medium. Return pork chops to skillet; spoon sauce over and simmer 1 minute.   *Makes 4 servings*

Prep and cook time: 20 minutes

Nutrients per serving: Calories: 304, Total Fat: 9 g, Protein: 16 g, Carbohydrate: 31 g, Cholesterol: 53 mg, Sodium: 92 mg, Dietary Fiber: 1 g
Dietary Exchanges: Fruit: 2, Meat: 2½, Fat: 1

PASTA PRIMAVERA

8 ounces uncooked mafalde pasta

2 medium zucchini (about 1 pound)

3 tablespoons roasted garlic-flavored vegetable oil

1 red bell pepper, thinly sliced

½ cup loosely packed fresh basil leaves, coarsely chopped

½ cup grated Parmesan cheese

1. Cook pasta according to package directions; drain. Place in large bowl.

2. While pasta is cooking, cut zucchini lengthwise into halves. Cut crosswise into thin slices.

3. Heat oil in large skillet over medium-high heat until hot. Add zucchini and bell pepper; cook and stir 3 to 4 minutes or until vegetables are crisp-tender, stirring frequently.

4. Add zucchini mixture and basil to pasta; toss gently until well combined. Season to taste with salt and black pepper. Serve with cheese.   *Makes 4 servings*

Prep and cook time: 30 minutes

FOR A SPECIAL TOUCH, CUT BASIL LEAVES INTO THIN STRIPS BY STACKING LEAVES, ROLLING UP AND SLICING INTO STRIPS.

Nutrients per serving: Calories: 401, Total Fat: 15 g, Protein: 15 g, Carbohydrate: 52 g, Cholesterol: 10 mg, Sodium: 237 mg, Dietary Fiber: 2 g
Dietary Exchanges: Vegetable: 2, Bread: 3, Fat: 3

CORN BREAD STUFFING WITH SAUSAGE AND APPLE

⅓ cup pecan pieces
1 pound bulk pork sausage
1 large Jonathan apple
1⅓ cups chicken broth
¼ cup apple juice
6 ounces seasoned cornbread
   stuffing mix

1. Preheat oven to 300°F. Place nuts in shallow baking pan. Bake 6 to 8 minutes or until lightly browned, stirring frequently. Place sausage in large skillet; cook over high heat 10 minutes or until meat is no longer pink, breaking meat apart with wooden spoon. Pour off drippings.

2. While browning sausage, coarsely chop apple. Place in 3-quart saucepan. Add chicken broth, apple juice and seasoning packet from stuffing mix. Bring to a boil, uncovered, over high heat. Remove from heat and stir in stuffing mix. Cover and let stand 3 to 5 minutes or until stuffing is moist and tender. Stir sausage into stuffing. Spoon into serving bowl and top stuffing with nuts.

Makes 4 servings

Prep and cook time: 19 minutes

Nutrients per serving:
Calories: 460, Total Fat: 25 g,
Protein: 16 g, Carbohydrate: 42 g,
Cholesterol: 50 mg,
Sodium: 1569 mg,
Dietary Fiber: 1 g
Dietary Exchanges: Fruit: ½,
Bread: 2½, Meat: 1½, Fat: 4

EASY EASEL RECIPES

PASTA WITH SPINACH AND RICOTTA

8 ounces uncooked tri-colored rotini

1 box (10 ounces) frozen chopped spinach, thawed and drained

2 teaspoons bottled minced garlic

1 cup fat-free or part-skim ricotta cheese

3 tablespoons grated Parmesan cheese, divided

1. Cook pasta according to package directions; drain.

2. While pasta is cooking, coat skillet with nonstick cooking spray; heat over medium-low heat. Add spinach and garlic; cook and stir 5 minutes. Stir in ricotta cheese, half of Parmesan cheese and ½ cup water; season with salt and pepper to taste.

3. Add pasta to skillet; stir until well blended. Sprinkle with remaining Parmesan cheese.

Makes 4 servings

Prep and cook time: 24 minutes

Note: For extra flavor and color, add a chopped fresh tomato or a can of diced tomatoes to the skillet with the pasta.

For a special touch, garnish with fresh basil leaves.

Nutrients per serving:
Calories: 182, Total Fat: 4 g,
Protein: 16 g, Carbohydrate: 26 g,
Cholesterol: 4 mg,
Sodium: 179 mg,
Dietary Fiber: trace
Dietary Exchanges: Vegetable: 2,
Bread: 1, Meat: 1, Fat: 1

EASY EASEL RECIPES

HOMESTYLE POTATO PATTIES

½ **pound bulk sausage**

4 **cups frozen shredded potatoes**

⅓ **cup minced onion**

2 **eggs, lightly beaten**

½ **teaspoon chili powder**

3 **tablespoons vegetable oil, divided**

1. Crumble sausage into large skillet; brown over medium-high heat until no longer pink, stirring to separate meat. Drain sausage on paper towels and discard fat.

2. Combine sausage, potatoes, onion, eggs and chili powder in large bowl. Season with salt and pepper.

3. Heat 1 tablespoon oil in large skillet over medium heat until hot. Drop potato mixture by cupfuls into skillet, pressing mixture with spatula to form 3½-inch patties. Cook

5 minutes; turn and cook 2 minutes. Drain on paper towels. Repeat with remaining potato mixture, adding additional oil as needed. *Makes 4 servings*

Prep and cook time: 20 minutes

Nutrients per serving: Calories: 431, Total Fat: 21 g, Protein: 12 g, Carbohydrate: 49 g, Cholesterol: 129 mg, Sodium: 387 mg, Dietary Fiber: 3 g
Dietary Exchanges: Bread: 3, Meat: 1, Fat: 3½

. . . .

Cook's Notes:

Serve with barbecue sauce or salsa.

. . . .

CHEESY HERB-STUFFED MUSHROOMS WITH SPINACH FETTUCCINE

2 packages (9 ounces each) fresh spinach fettuccine
⅓ cup extra-virgin olive oil
1 tablespoon dried basil leaves
2 cloves garlic, minced
1 package (6½ ounces) garlic and herb soft spreadable cheese
16 large mushrooms, rinsed and stems removed

1. Prepare barbecue grill for direct cooking.

2. Cook fettuccine according to package directions. Drain; return to saucepan.

3. Meanwhile, combine oil, basil and garlic in small bowl; pour over cooked pasta. Toss well; set aside.

4. Cut aluminum foil into 4 large squares. Spoon about 1 tablespoon cheese into each mushroom cap. Place four mushroom caps, cheese sides up, in center of each square.

Fold aluminum foil to close, leaving small air pocket directly above cheese.

5. Place packets on grid. Grill, on covered grill, over hot coals 5 minutes or until mushroom caps are fork-tender. Remove from grill.

6. Transfer fettuccine to serving bowl. Remove mushroom caps from packets; arrange over fettuccine. Serve immediately.

Makes 4 to 6 servings

Prep and cook time: 30 minutes

Nutrients per serving: Calories: 736, Total Fat: 36 g, Protein: 26 g, Carbohydrate: 77 g, Cholesterol: 32 mg, Sodium: 1270 mg, Dietary Fiber: 3 g
Dietary Exchanges: Bread: 5, Meat: 1½, Fat: 6

BRATWURST SKILLET BREAKFAST

1½ **pounds red potatoes**
3 **bratwurst links (about ¾ pound)**
2 **tablespoons butter or margarine**
1½ **teaspoons caraway seeds**
4 **cups shredded red cabbage**

1. Cut potatoes into ¼- to ½-inch pieces. Place in microwavable casserole. Microwave, covered, on HIGH 3 minutes; stir. Microwave 2 minutes more or until just tender; set aside.

2. While potatoes are cooking, slice bratwurst into ¼-inch pieces. Place bratwurst in large skillet; cook over medium-high heat, stirring occasionally, 8 minutes or until browned and no longer pink in center. Remove bratwurst from pan with slotted spoon; set aside. Pour off drippings.

3. Melt butter in skillet. Add potatoes and caraway. Cook, stirring occasionally, 6 to 8 minutes or until potatoes are golden and tender. Return bratwurst to skillet; stir in cabbage. Cook, covered, 3 minutes or until cabbage is slightly wilted. Uncover and stir 3 to 4 minutes more or until cabbage is just tender yet still bright red.

Makes 4 servings

Prep and cook time: 30 minutes

SERVING SUGGESTION: *Serve with fresh fruit and English muffin.*

Nutrients per serving:
Calories: 459, Total Fat: 28 g,
Protein: 16 g, Carbohydrate: 37 g,
Cholesterol: 66 mg,
Sodium: 548 mg,
Dietary Fiber: 1 g
Dietary Exchanges: Vegetable: 1,
Bread: 2, Meat: 2, Fat: 4

SKILLET PESTO TORTELLINI

1 ¼ cups milk
1 envelope (1.2 ounces) creamy pesto
 sauce mix
1 package (16 ounces) frozen vegetable
 medley
1 package (12 ounces) frozen tortellini
 Dash ground red pepper
½ cup (2 ounces) shredded mozzarella
 cheese

3. Sprinkle with cheese just before serving.

Makes 4 servings

Prep and cook time: 22 minutes

SERVING SUGGESTION: *For a complete meal,
serve with dinner rolls, mixed green salad and
orange sorbet for dessert.*

*Nutrients per serving: Calories: 306, Total Fat: 12 g,
Protein: 15 g, Carbohydrate: 34 g, Cholesterol: 68 mg,
Sodium: 866 mg, Dietary Fiber: 5 g
Dietary Exchanges: Vegetable: 1, Bread: 2, Meat: 1, Fat: 2*

1. Blend 1 ¼ cups water, milk and sauce mix
in large deep skillet. Bring to a boil over high
heat. Stir in vegetables,
tortellini and ground red
pepper; return to a boil.

2. Cook vegetables and
tortellini, uncovered, over
medium-high heat 8 to
10 minutes or until
tortellini is tender and
sauce has thickened,
stirring occasionally.

EASY EASEL RECIPES

BRATWURST SKILLET

1 pound bratwurst links, cut into
   ½-inch slices
1½ cups green bell pepper strips
1½ cups red bell pepper strips
1½ cups sliced onions
1 teaspoon paprika
1 teaspoon caraway seeds

1. Heat large skillet over medium heat until hot. Add bratwurst; cover and cook about 5 minutes or until browned and no longer pink in center. Transfer bratwurst to plate. Cover and keep warm.

2. Drain all but 1 tablespoon drippings from skillet. Add bell peppers, onions, paprika and caraway seeds. Cook and stir about 5 minutes or until vegetables are tender.

3. Combine bratwurst and vegetables. Serve immediately. *Makes 4 servings*

Prep and cook time: 18 minutes

Nutrients per serving: Calories: 419, Total Fat: 30 g, Protein: 19 g, Carbohydrate: 20 g, Cholesterol: 68 mg, Sodium: 635 mg, Dietary Fiber: 4 g
Dietary Exchanges: Vegetable: 3, Meat: 2½, Fat: 4½

◤ C U T T I N G   C O R N E R S :

To make this even speedier, purchase a packaged stir-fry pepper and onion mix and use in place of the bell peppers and onions.

EASY EASEL RECIPES

QUATTRO FORMAGGIO PIZZA

1 (12-inch) Italian bread shell
½ cup pizza or marinara sauce
¼ pound shaved or thinly sliced provolone cheese
1 cup (4 ounces) shredded smoked or regular mozzarella cheese
⅛ pound thinly sliced brick cheese
¼ cup freshly grated Parmesan or Romano cheese

1. Preheat oven to 450°F.

2. Place bread shell on baking sheet. Spread pizza sauce evenly over shell.

3. Top sauce with provolone, mozzarella, brick and Parmesan cheeses.

4. Bake 14 minutes or until bread shell is golden brown and cheeses are melted.

5. Cut into wedges; serve immediately.

Makes 4 servings

Prep and cook time: 26 minutes

SERVING SUGGESTION: *Serve Quattro Formaggio Pizza with a mixed green and tomato salad.*

Nutrients per serving: Calories: 600, Total Fat: 27 g, Protein: 34 g, Carbohydrate: 54 g, Cholesterol: 65 mg, Sodium: 1465 mg, Dietary Fiber: trace
Dietary Exchanges: Vegetable: 1, Bread: 4, Meat: 2½, Fat: 3½

CUTTING CORNERS:
To save time in the kitchen, purchase the provolone, mozzarella and brick cheese at the deli counter and have them slice it for you.

EASY EASEL RECIPES

BREAKFAST PIZZA

1 can (10 ounces) refrigerated pizza dough

1 package (7 ounces) pre-browned fully cooked sausage patties, thawed

3 eggs

½ cup milk

1 teaspoon dried Italian seasoning

2 cups (8 ounces) shredded pizza-style cheese

1. Preheat oven to 425°F. For crust, unroll pizza dough and pat onto bottom and up side of greased 12-inch pizza pan. Bake 5 minutes or until set, but not browned.

2. While crust is baking, cut sausages into ½-inch pieces. Whisk together eggs, milk and Italian seasoning in bowl until well blended. Season with salt and pepper.

3. Spoon sausages over crust; sprinkle with cheese. Carefully pour egg mixture over sausage and cheese. Bake 15 to 20 minutes or until egg mixture is set and crust is golden. *Makes 6 servings*

Prep and cook time: 27 minutes

FOR A SPECIAL TOUCH, SERVE WITH YOUR FAVORITE SALSA.

Nutrients per serving: Calories: 385, Total Fat: 20 g, Protein: 25 g, Carbohydrate: 25 g, Cholesterol: 148 mg, Sodium: 910 mg, Dietary Fiber: 0 g
Dietary Exchanges: Bread: 1½, Meat: 3, Fat: 2½

GRILLED VEGETABLE SANDWICHES WITH GARLIC MAYONNAISE

⅓ **cup mayonnaise**

2 **cloves garlic, minced**

2 **large red bell peppers, cored and quartered**

1 **small eggplant, cut into ¼-inch slices Vegetable oil**

8 **slices country-style bread**

1. Prepare barbecue grill for direct cooking.

2. Blend mayonnaise and garlic in small bowl; set aside.

3. Spray barbecue grid with nonstick cooking spray. Place bell peppers and eggplant on prepared grid. Brush vegetables with oil; season with salt and black pepper to taste.

4. Grill vegetables, on covered grill, over medium-hot coals 10 minutes or until fork-tender, turning halfway through grilling time.

5. Spread desired amount of Garlic Mayonnaise on each bread slice. Top 4 bread slices with equal amounts of grilled vegetables; cover with remaining bread. Cut each sandwich in half. Serve immediately.

Makes 4 servings

Prep and cook time: 25 minutes

Nutrients per serving:
Calories: 453, Total Fat: 21 g,
Protein: 9 g, Carbohydrate: 57 g,
Cholesterol: 9 mg,
Sodium: 398 mg,
Dietary Fiber: 2 g
Dietary Exchanges: Vegetable: 4,
Bread: 2, Fat: 4

EASY EASEL RECIPES

ITALIAN SAUSAGE AND VEGETABLE STEW

1 pound hot or mild Italian sausage, cut into 1-inch pieces

1 package (16 ounces) frozen mixed vegetables (onions and green, red and yellow peppers)

2 medium zucchini, sliced

4 cloves garlic, minced

1 can (14½ ounces) diced Italian-style tomatoes, undrained

1 jar (14½ ounces) sliced mushrooms, drained

1. Cook sausage in large saucepan, covered, over medium to medium-high heat 5 minutes or until browned; pour off drippings.

2. Add frozen vegetables, zucchini, garlic, tomatoes and mushrooms; bring to a boil. Reduce heat to low;

simmer, covered, 10 minutes. Cook uncovered 5 to 10 minutes or until juices have thickened slightly.   *Makes 6 (1-cup) servings*

Prep and cook time: 30 minutes

SERVING SUGGESTION: *Italian Sausage and Vegetable Stew is excellent served with garlic bread.*

Nutrients per serving: Calories: 234, Total Fat: 15 g, Protein: 14 g, Carbohydrate: 12 g, Cholesterol: 43 mg, Sodium: 732 mg, Dietary Fiber: 2 g
Dietary Exchanges: Vegetable: 2, Meat: 2, Fat: 1½

EASY EASEL RECIPES

GRILLED VEGETABLE & CHEESE SANDWICHES

2 large zucchini squash, cut lengthwise into eight ¼-inch slices
4 slices sweet onion (such as Vidalia or Walla Walla) cut ¼ inch thick
1 large yellow bell pepper, cut lengthwise into quarters
6 tablespoons prepared light or regular Caesar salad dressing, divided
8 oval slices sourdough bread
6 (1-ounce) slices Muenster cheese

1. Prepare barbecue for grilling. Brush both sides of vegetables with ¼ cup dressing. Place vegetables on grid over medium coals. Grill on covered grill 5 minutes. Turn; grill 2 minutes.

2. Brush both sides of bread lightly with remaining 2 tablespoons dressing. Place bread around vegetables; grill 2 minutes or until bread is lightly toasted. Turn bread; top 4 pieces of bread with 4 slices of cheese. Tear remaining 2 cheese slices into small pieces; place on bread around cheese. Grill vegetables and bread 1 to 2 minutes more or until cheese is melted, bread is toasted and vegetables are crisp-tender.

3. Arrange vegetables over cheese side of bread; top with remaining bread.

Makes 4 servings

Prep and cook time: 22 minutes

SERVING SUGGESTION: *Serve with a fresh fruit salad.*

Nutrients per serving: Calories: 349, Total Fat: 16 g, Protein: 16 g, Carbohydrate: 36 g, Cholesterol: 48 mg, Sodium: 716 mg, Dietary Fiber: 1 g
Dietary Exchanges: Vegetable: 1, Meat: 1½, Fat: 2

MUFFULETTA

1 (12-ounce) loaf focaccia bread
3 tablespoons prepared Italian salad
   dressing
½ cup sliced Spanish olives
8 ounces thinly sliced salami or
   baked ham
4 ounces thinly sliced provolone or
   sharp Cheddar cheese
Lettuce leaves

*Nutrients per serving: Calories: 609, Total Fat: 36 g,
Protein: 24 g, Carbohydrate: 48 g, Cholesterol: 64 mg,
Sodium: 2158 mg, Dietary Fiber: 0 g
Dietary Exchanges: Bread: 4, Meat: 3, Fat: 3½*

LIGHTEN UP:
*To reduce the amount of fat in this recipe,
replace the Italian salad dressing with
reduced-fat or fat-free Italian salad dressing.*

1. Cut bread crosswise into halves; brush cut
sides of both halves generously with salad
dressing. Pour any remaining salad dressing
over olives.

2. Arrange meat and
cheese on bottom half of
bread; top with olives,
lettuce leaves and top half
of bread. Cut into 4 wedges
to serve.

Makes 4 servings

Prep time: 12 minutes

CARPACCIO DI ZUCCHINI

¾ **pound zucchini, shredded**
½ **cup sliced almonds, toasted**
 1 **tablespoon Italian salad dressing**
 4 **French bread baguettes, sliced in half lengthwise**
 4 **teaspoons soft spread margarine**
 3 **tablespoons grated Parmesan cheese**

1. Preheat broiler. Place zucchini in bowl. Add almonds and dressing; mix well. Set aside.

2. Place baguette halves on large baking sheet; spread evenly with margarine. Sprinkle with cheese. Broil 3 inches from heat 2 to 3 minutes or until edges and cheese are browned.

3. Spread zucchini mixture evenly on each baguette half. Serve immediately.

Makes 4 servings

Prep and cook time: 28 minutes

FOR A SPECIAL TOUCH, GARNISH CARPACCIO WITH CHERRY TOMATO HALVES.

Nutrients per serving: Calories: 180, Total Fat: 15 g, Protein: 6 g, Carbohydrate: 6 g, Cholesterol: 4 mg, Sodium: 305 mg, Dietary Fiber: 2 g
Dietary Exchanges: Vegetable: 1, Meat: ½, Fat: 3

Serve It With Style!

Serve this tasty open-faced sandwich with penne smothered in a spicy marinara sauce.

EASY EASEL RECIPES

MACARONI AND CHEESE PRONTO

8 ounces uncooked elbow macaroni
1 can (10¾ ounces) cream of
   Cheddar soup
½ cup milk
2 cups diced cooked ham (about
   ½ pound)
1 cup (4 ounces) shredded Cheddar
   cheese
½ cup frozen peas

1. Cook macaroni according to package directions. Drain and set aside.

2. While macaroni is cooking, combine soup and milk in large saucepan. Cook and stir over medium heat until smooth.

3. Add ham, cheese, peas and cooked macaroni to soup mixture. Reduce heat to low, cooking and stirring 5 minutes or until cheese melts and mixture is heated through. Add pepper to taste.

Makes 4 servings

Prep and cook time: 20 minutes

FOR A SPECIAL TOUCH, GARNISH MACARONI AND CHEESE PRONTO WITH FRESH ITALIAN PARSLEY BEFORE SERVING.

Nutrients per serving: Calories: 494, Total Fat: 14 g, Protein: 33 g, Carbohydrate: 56 g, Cholesterol: 63 mg, Sodium: 1513 mg, Dietary Fiber: 1 g
Dietary Exchanges: Bread: 4, Meat: 2, Fat: 2

Cook's Notes:
Perfectly cooked pasta should be al dente—tender but still firm to the bite. Test your pasta shortly before the time recommended on the package to avoid overcooking.

POTATO-ZUCCHINI PANCAKES

1 medium Idaho or russet potato,
   unpeeled and shredded
½ small zucchini, shredded
1 green onion, thinly sliced
1 egg white
2 tablespoons all-purpose flour
1 tablespoon vegetable oil

1. Combine potato, zucchini, onion, egg white and flour in medium bowl until well blended. Add salt and pepper to taste.

2. Heat oil in large skillet over medium heat. Drop potato mixture into skillet by ⅓ cupfuls. Flatten pancakes with spatula; cook about 5 minutes per side or until browned.

   Makes 2 servings
   (3 pancakes per serving)

Prep and cook time:
18 minutes

Nutrients per serving: Calories: 167, Total Fat: 7 g,
Protein: 4 g, Carbohydrate: 23 g, Cholesterol: 0 mg,
Sodium: 33 mg, Dietary Fiber: trace
Dietary Exchanges: Bread: 1½, Fat: 1½

CUTTING CORNERS:

Save time by shredding both the potato and zucchini in a food processor fitted with a shredding disc. There's no need to wash the bowl in between because all the ingredients are mixed together before cooking.

EASY EASEL RECIPES

HAM STROMBOLI

1 can (10 ounces) refrigerated pizza
    dough
1 tablespoon prepared mustard
½ pound thinly sliced deli ham
1 package (3½ ounces) sliced pepperoni
1 teaspoon dried Italian seasoning
2 cups (8 ounces) shredded part-skim
    mozzarella cheese

1. Preheat oven to 425°F. Unroll pizza dough on greased jelly-roll pan; pat dough into 12-inch square. Spread mustard over dough to within ½ inch of edges. Layer ham slices down center 6 inches of dough, leaving 3-inch border on either side and ½-inch border at top and bottom. Top ham with pepperoni slices. Sprinkle with Italian seasoning and cheese.

2. Fold sides of dough over filling, pinching center seam and top and bottom to seal. Bake 15 to 20 minutes or until lightly browned.

Makes 6 servings

Prep and cook time: 22 minutes

Nutrients per serving: Calories: 341, Total Fat: 16 g, Protein: 25 g, Carbohydrate: 25 g, Cholesterol: 43 mg, Sodium: 117 mg, Dietary Fiber: 1 g
Dietary Exchanges: Bread: 1½, Meat: 3, Fat: 1½

Serve It With Style!

To make this meal complete, just add a tossed salad and fresh fruit for dessert.

CHICK-PEA PATTIES

1 **can (15 ounces) chick-peas (garbanzo beans), rinsed and drained**
1 **cup shredded carrots**
⅓ **cup seasoned dry bread crumbs**
2 **tablespoons creamy Italian salad dressing**
1 **egg**
2 **tablespoons vegetable oil**

1. Mash chick-peas coarsely in medium bowl with hand potato masher, leaving some larger pieces. Stir in carrots, bread crumbs, dressing and egg.

2. Shape chick-pea mixture into 4 patties.

3. Heat oil in large nonstick skillet over medium-high heat. Add patties; cook 3 minutes per side or until well-browned.

4. Remove from skillet using spatula; drain on paper towels. Serve immediately.

Makes 4 servings

Prep and cook time: 18 minutes

Nutrients per serving: Calories: 266, Total Fat: 14 g, Protein: 8 g, Carbohydrate: 28 g, Cholesterol: 53 mg, Sodium: 771 mg, Dietary Fiber: 6 g
Dietary Exchanges: Bread: 2, Fat: 2½

Cook's Notes:

Chick-peas are slightly larger than the average green peas, and have a round, irregular shape. They have a firm texture and mild nutlike flavor.

EASY EASEL RECIPES

POLYNESIAN HAM STEAK AND GLAZED VEGETABLES

1 **can (8 ounces) pineapple chunks in juice, undrained**
1 **tablespoon plus 1½ teaspoons cornstarch**
¼ **cup packed light brown sugar**
3 **tablespoons cider vinegar**
1 **green bell pepper, seeded and chopped**
¾ **pound deli honey cured or smoked center cut ham slice, cut ½ inch thick**

1. Drain pineapple, reserving juice. Stir cornstarch into reserved juice, mixing until smooth.

2. Combine juice mixture, brown sugar and vinegar in large nonstick skillet. Cook over medium heat 2 minutes or until mixture thickens, stirring constantly. Stir in bell pepper. Add ham.

3. Cover and cook 5 minutes. Turn ham, stirring in reserved pineapple chunks. Cover and cook 4 to 5 minutes or until ham is heated through and glaze is thickened.

Makes 4 servings

Prep and cook time: 25 minutes

Nutrients per serving: Calories: 196, Total Fat: 2 g, Protein: 16 g, Carbohydrate: 30 g, Cholesterol: 39 mg, Sodium: 857 mg, Dietary Fiber: 1 g Dietary Exchanges: Fruit: 1½, Meat: 2

CUTTING CORNERS: Canned fruits can offer an amazing amount of time-saving convenience in the kitchen. There's no need to peel, clean or chop fresh fruits.

EASY EASEL RECIPES

THE MEATLESS DAGWOOD

¾ **pound deli egg salad**

¼ **cup coarsely chopped pitted kalamata olives or ripe olives**

6 **slices marble rye or pumpernickel bread**

4 **thin slices (2 ounces) brick or provolone cheese**

2 **dill pickles, thinly sliced**

2 **romaine or red leaf lettuce leaves**

1. Combine egg salad and olives in small bowl.

2. Layer sandwich ingredients as follows: 1 slice bread, 1 slice cheese, ¼ egg-olive mixture, 1 pickle slice, 1 slice bread, 1 lettuce leaf, 1 slice cheese, ¼ egg-olive mixture, and 1 slice bread.

3. Repeat to make a second sandwich. Serve immediately.   *Makes 2 servings*

Prep time: 10 minutes

Nutrients per serving: Calories: 788, Total Fat: 50 g, Protein: 31 g, Carbohydrate: 56 g, Cholesterol: 587 mg, Sodium: 3107 mg, Dietary Fiber: 2 g
Dietary Exchanges: Bread: 3½, Meat: 3, Fat: 8

CUTTING CORNERS:

To save time, purchase dill pickles that are already sliced for sandwiches.

BAKED EGGS FLORENTINE

2 packages (10 ounces each) frozen creamed spinach
4 slices (⅛ inch thick) deli ham, about 5 to 6 ounces
4 eggs
⅛ teaspoon ground nutmeg
½ cup (2 ounces) shredded provolone cheese
2 tablespoons chopped roasted red pepper

1. Preheat oven to 450°F. Make small cut in each package of spinach. Microwave on HIGH 5 to 6 minutes, turning packages halfway through cooking time.

2. Grease 8-inch square pan. Place ham slices on bottom of pan, overlapping slightly. Spread spinach mixture over ham slices.

3. Make 4 indentations in spinach. Carefully place 1 egg in each indentation. Season to taste with salt and black pepper. Sprinkle with nutmeg.

4. Bake 16 to 19 minutes or until eggs are set. Remove from oven. Sprinkle cheese and red pepper over top. Return to oven; bake 1 to 2 minutes longer or until cheese is melted. Serve immediately.

Makes 4 servings

Prep and cook time: 28 minutes

SERVING SUGGESTION:
Serve with toasted English muffin halves and fresh pineapple pieces.

Nutrients per serving:
Calories: 254, Total Fat: 14 g,
Protein: 21 g, Carbohydrate: 15 g,
Cholesterol: 246 mg,
Sodium: 1163 mg,
Dietary Fiber: 3 g
Dietary Exchanges: Vegetable: 3,
Meat: 2, Fat: 1½

EASY EASEL
RECIPES

EASY VEGGIE-TOPPED BAKED SPUDS

2½ **cups frozen broccoli-carrot vegetable medley**
4 **large baking potatoes**
1 **can (10¾ ounces) cream of broccoli soup**
½ **cup (2 ounces) shredded Cheddar cheese**

1. Place frozen vegetables in microwavable bowl. Microwave on HIGH 5 minutes; drain.

2. Scrub potatoes; pierce several times with knife. Microwave on HIGH 15 minutes or until potatoes are softened.

3. While potatoes are cooking, combine soup, vegetables and cheese in medium saucepan. Cook and stir over low heat

until cheese melts and mixture is heated through. Split baked potatoes in half. Top each potato with soup mixture. Add salt and pepper to taste.   *Makes 4 servings*

Prep and cook time: 23 minutes

Nutrients per serving: Calories: 351, Total Fat: 6 g,
Protein: 11 g, Carbohydrate: 65 g, Cholesterol: 15 mg,
Sodium: 675 mg, Dietary Fiber: 2 g
Dietary Exchanges: Vegetable: 1, Bread: 4, Fat: 1

Cook's Notes:
Choose russet or Idaho potatoes for baking. Store them in a cool, dark place away from onions for up to 2 weeks. (Storing potatoes and onions together will cause the potatoes to rot more quickly.)

BRUNSWICK STEW

12 ounces smoked ham or cooked chicken breast, cut into ¾- to 1-inch cubes

1 cup sliced onion

4½ teaspoons all-purpose flour

1 can (14½ ounces) stewed tomatoes, undrained

2 cups frozen mixed vegetables for soup (such as okra, lima beans, potatoes, celery, corn, carrots, green beans and onions)

1 cup chicken broth

1. Spray saucepan with nonstick cooking spray; heat over medium heat until hot. Add ham and onion; cook 5 minutes or until ham is browned. Stir in flour; cook over medium to medium-low heat 1 minute, stirring constantly.

2. Stir in tomatoes, mixed vegetables and broth, bringing to a boil. Reduce heat to low; simmer, covered, 5 to 8 minutes or until vegetables are tender. Simmer, uncovered, 5 to 8 minutes or until slightly thickened. Season to taste with salt and pepper.

Makes 4 (1-cup) servings

Prep and cook time: 30 minutes

SERVING SUGGESTION: *Brunswick Stew is excellent served over rice or squares of cornbread.*

Nutrients per serving:
Calories: 194, Total Fat: 3 g,
Protein: 22 g, Carbohydrate: 25 g,
Cholesterol: 53 mg,
Sodium: 1533 mg,
Dietary Fiber: 4 g
Dietary Exchanges: Vegetable: 2,
Bread: 1, Meat: 2

EASY EASEL RECIPES

Quick Vegetarian

Pasta with Spinach and Ricotta (page 92)

Pronto Poultry

Grilled Ginger Chicken with Pineapple and Coconut Rice (page 57)

ISLA MUJERES SHRIMP PIZZA

1 **bread-style prepared pizza crust (12 inches)**

¼ to ½ **cup prepared salsa**

2 **cups (8 ounces) shredded Monterey Jack or taco-seasoned cheese**

1 **bag (8 ounces) frozen cooked shrimp, thawed and well drained**

1 **small tomato, seeded and chopped**

2 **tablespoons chopped cilantro**

Nutrients per serving: Calories: 592, Total Fat: 24 g, Protein: 40 g, Carbohydrate: 51 g, Cholesterol: 166 mg, Sodium: 1145 mg, Dietary Fiber: 1 g
Dietary Exchanges: Vegetable: 1, Bread: 3, Meat: 5, Fat: 2

Cook's Notes:

You can vary the heat level of the Isla Mujeres Shrimp Pizza by using different varieties of salsa. Mild, medium and hot salsa are all available at the supermarket.

1. Preheat oven to 450°F.

2. Layer pizza crust with salsa, half of cheese, shrimp, tomato and cilantro. Sprinkle with remaining cheese.

3. Bake 10 minutes or until cheese is melted and bubbly.

Makes 4 to 6 servings

Prep and cook time:
15 minutes

GAZEBO CHICKEN

4 boneless chicken breast halves (about 1½ pounds)

6 cups torn butter lettuce leaves or mixed baby greens

1 ripe cantaloupe, seeded and cut into 12 wedges

1 large carrot, shredded

½ cup (3 ounces) fresh raspberries

⅔ cup honey-mustard salad dressing, divided

1. Preheat broiler. Place chicken, skin side down, on broiler pan rack. Season with salt and pepper to taste. Broil 4 to 5 inches from heat 8 minutes. Turn; sprinkle with salt and pepper. Broil 6 to 8 minutes or until chicken is no longer pink in center. Remove to cutting board; cool.

2. Place lettuce on large serving platter; arrange cantaloupe and carrot around lettuce.

3. Slice each chicken breast diagonally into fourths; place over lettuce.

4. Arrange raspberries over salad; drizzle with 2 tablespoons dressing. Serve with remaining dressing. *Makes 4 servings*

Prep and cook time: 25 minutes

SERVING SUGGESTION: *Serve salad with corn muffins and herb-flavored butter.*

Nutrients per serving:
Calories: 465, Total Fat: 21 g,
Protein: 40 g, Carbohydrate: 29 g,
Cholesterol: 103 mg,
Sodium: 332 mg, Dietary Fiber: 3 g
Dietary Exchanges: Fruit: 2,
Meat: 4, Fat: 2

JAMAICAN SHRIMP & PINEAPPLE KABOBS

½ **cup prepared jerk sauce**

¼ **cup pineapple preserves**

2 **tablespoons minced fresh chives**

1 **pound large shrimp, peeled and deveined**

½ **medium pineapple, peeled, cored and cut into 1-inch cubes**

2 **large red, green or yellow bell peppers, cut into 1-inch cubes**

1. Combine jerk sauce, preserves and chives in small bowl; mix well. Thread shrimp, pineapple and peppers onto 4 metal skewers; brush with jerk sauce mixture.

2. Grill kabobs over medium-hot coals 6 to 10 minutes or until shrimp turn pink and opaque, turning once. Serve with remaining jerk sauce mixture.

Makes 4 servings

Prep and cook time: 25 minutes

SERVING SUGGESTION: *Serve kabobs with hot cooked rice.*

Nutrients per serving: Calories: 226, Total Fat: 3 g, Protein: 20 g, Carbohydrate: 31 g, Cholesterol: 175 mg, Sodium: 262 mg, Dietary Fiber: 2 g
Dietary Exchanges: Vegetable: 1, Fruit: 1½, Meat: 2½

CUTTING CORNERS:
Purchase pineapple already trimmed and cored in the produce section of your local supermarket.

BLACK AND WHITE CHILI

1 **pound chicken tenders, cut into ¾-inch pieces**
1 **cup coarsely chopped onion**
1 **can (15½ ounces) Great Northern beans, drained**
1 **can (15 ounces) black beans, drained**
1 **can (14½ ounces) Mexican-style stewed tomatoes, undrained**
2 **tablespoons Texas-style chili powder seasoning mix**

1. Spray large saucepan with nonstick cooking spray; heat over medium heat until hot. Add chicken and onion; cook and stir over medium to medium-high heat 5 to 8 minutes or until chicken is browned.

2. Stir remaining ingredients into

saucepan; bring to a boil. Reduce heat to low; simmer, uncovered, 10 minutes.

Makes 6 (1-cup) servings

Prep and cook time: 30 minutes

Nutrients per serving: Calories: 268, Total Fat: 3 g, Protein: 29 g, Carbohydrate: 36 g, Cholesterol: 46 mg, Sodium: 401 mg, Dietary Fiber: 6 g
Dietary Exchanges: Vegetable: 1, Bread: 2, Meat: 2

Serve It With Style!

For a change of pace, this delicious chili is excellent served over cooked rice or pasta.

GRILLED ORIENTAL SHRIMP KABOBS

ORIENTAL MARINADE

> 3 tablespoons soy sauce or reduced-sodium soy sauce
> 1 tablespoon regular or seasoned rice vinegar
> 1 tablespoon Oriental sesame oil
> 2 cloves garlic, minced
> ¼ teaspoon red pepper flakes

SHRIMP KABOBS

> 1 pound uncooked large shrimp, peeled and deveined

1. For marinade, combine soy sauce, vinegar, oil, garlic and pepper flakes in small bowl; mix well. Cover; refrigerate up to 3 days.

2. Combine marinade and shrimp in resealable plastic food storage bag. Seal bag securely. Refrigerate at least 30 minutes or up to 2 hours, turning bag once.

3. To complete recipe, spray barbecue grid with nonstick cooking spray. Prepare barbecue grill for direct cooking.

4. Drain shrimp, reserving marinade. Thread shrimp onto 4 (12-inch) skewers. Place skewers on prepared grid; brush with half of reserved marinade. Grill skewers, on covered grill, over medium coals 5 minutes. Turn skewers; brush with remaining half of marinade. Grill 3 to 5 minutes or until shrimp turn pink and opaque.

Makes 4 servings

Make-ahead time: 2 hours or up to 3 days in refrigerator

Final prep and cook time: 20 minutes

SERVING SUGGESTION: *Serve with vegetable fried rice and fresh pineapple spears.*

Nutrients per serving: Calories: 129, Total Fat: 4 g, Protein: 19 g, Carbohydrate: 2 g, Cholesterol: 175 mg, Sodium: 971 mg, Dietary Fiber: trace Dietary Exchanges: Meat: 2½

EASY EASEL™ RECIPES

GRILLED ROSEMARY CHICKEN

2 tablespoons lemon juice
2 tablespoons olive oil
2 cloves garlic, minced
2 tablespoons minced fresh rosemary
¼ teaspoon salt
4 boneless skinless chicken breasts

1. Whisk together lemon juice, oil, garlic, rosemary and salt in small bowl. Pour into shallow glass dish. Add chicken, turning to coat both sides with lemon juice mixture. Cover and marinate in refrigerator 15 minutes, turning chicken once.

2. Grill chicken over medium-hot coals 5 to 6 minutes per side or until chicken is no longer pink in center.

Makes 4 servings

Prep and cook time:
30 minutes

Nutrients per serving: Calories: 156, Total Fat: 5 g, Protein: 25 g, Carbohydrate: trace, Cholesterol: 69 mg, Sodium: 104 mg, Dietary Fiber: trace
Dietary Exchanges: Meat: 3

Cook's Notes:

For added flavor, moisten a few sprigs of fresh rosemary and toss on the hot coals just before grilling. Store rosemary in the refrigerator for up to 5 days. Wrap sprigs in a barely damp paper towel and place in a sealed plastic bag.

CREOLE SHRIMP AND RICE

2 tablespoons olive oil
1 cup uncooked white rice
**1 can (15 ounces) diced tomatoes with
    garlic, undrained**
**1 teaspoon Creole or Cajun seasoning
    blend**
1 pound peeled cooked medium shrimp
**1 package (10 ounces) frozen okra *or*
    1½ cups frozen sugar snap peas,
    thawed**

1. Heat oil in large skillet over medium heat until hot. Add rice; cook and stir 2 to 3 minutes or until lightly browned.

2. Add tomatoes with juice, 1½ cups water and seasoning blend; bring to a boil over high heat. Reduce heat to low. Cover; simmer 15 minutes.

3. Add shrimp and okra. Cook, covered, 3 minutes or until heated through.

Makes 4 servings

Prep and cook time: 20 minutes

*Nutrients per serving: Calories: 386, Total Fat: 9 g,
Protein: 29 g, Carbohydrate: 47 g, Cholesterol: 222 mg,
Sodium: 657 mg, Dietary Fiber: 1 g
Dietary Exchanges: Vegetable: 2, Bread: 2½, Meat: 3*

Cook's Notes:

**Okra are oblong, green pods. When cooked, it gives
off a viscous substance that acts as a good thickener.**

CHICKEN CACCIATORE

8 ounces dry noodles
1 can (15 ounces) chunky Italian-style tomato sauce
1 cup chopped green bell pepper
1 cup sliced onion
1 cup sliced mushrooms
4 boneless skinless chicken breast halves (1 pound)

1. Cook noodles according to package directions; drain.

2. While noodles are cooking, combine tomato sauce, bell pepper, onion and mushrooms in microwavable dish. Cover loosely with plastic wrap or waxed paper; microwave on HIGH 6 to 8 minutes, stirring halfway through cooking time.

3. While sauce mixture is cooking, coat large skillet with nonstick cooking spray and heat over medium-high heat. Cook chicken breasts 3 to 4 minutes per side or until lightly browned.

4. Add sauce mixture to skillet with salt and pepper to taste. Reduce heat to medium and simmer 12 to 15 minutes. Serve over noodles.   ***Makes 4 servings***

Prep and cook time: 30 minutes

Nutrients per serving:
Calories: 392, Total Fat: 5 g,
Protein: 35 g, Carbohydrate: 52 g,
Cholesterol: 118 mg,
Sodium: 633 mg,
Dietary Fiber: 4 g
Dietary Exchanges: Bread: 2,
Meat: 3

EASY EASEL RECIPES

RED SNAPPER WITH LIME-GINGER BUTTER

5 tablespoons butter, cut into small pieces
1 tablespoon bottled lime juice
3 cloves garlic
2 teaspoons ground ginger
½ teaspoon hot pepper sauce
6 red snapper fillets (about 1½ pounds)

1. Preheat broiler.

2. Combine butter, lime juice, garlic, ginger, pepper sauce, salt and pepper to taste in food processor; process until smooth paste forms.

3. Broil red snapper 4 to 5 inches from heat 5 minutes. Turn fillets over and broil 4 minutes more.

4. Place about 1 tablespoon lime-ginger butter on top of each fillet; broil 45 seconds. Serve immediately. *Makes 6 servings*

Prep and cook time: 18 minutes

FOR A SPECIAL TOUCH, SERVE FISH WITH RICE AND GARNISH WITH FRESH LIME SLICES AND CHIVES.

Nutrients per serving: Calories: 306, Total Fat: 12 g, Protein: 45 g, Carbohydrate: trace, Cholesterol: 106 mg, Sodium: 193 mg, Dietary Fiber: 0 g
Dietary Exchanges: Meat: 5½

Cook's Notes:
Halibut or swordfish can be substituted for the red snapper.

EASY EASEL RECIPES

SPICY CHICKEN STROMBOLI

1 cup frozen broccoli florets, thawed
1 can (10 ounces) diced chicken
1½ cups (6 ounces) shredded Monterey Jack cheese with jalapeños
¼ cup chunky salsa
2 green onions, chopped
1 can (10 ounces) refrigerated pizza dough

1. Preheat oven to 400°F. Coarsely chop broccoli. Combine broccoli, chicken, cheese, salsa and green onions in small bowl.

2. Unroll pizza dough. Pat into 15×10-inch rectangle. Sprinkle broccoli mixture evenly over top. Starting with long side, tightly roll into log jelly-roll style. Pinch seam to seal. Place on baking sheet, seam side down.

3. Bake 15 to 20 minutes or until golden brown. Transfer to wire rack to cool slightly. Slice and serve warm. *Makes 6 servings*

Prep and cook time: 30 minutes

SERVING SUGGESTION: *Serve with salsa on the side for dipping or pour salsa on top of slices for a boost of added flavor.*

Nutrients per serving: Calories: 311, Total Fat: 14 g, Protein: 22 g, Carbohydrate: 23 g, Cholesterol: 51 mg, Sodium: 723 mg, Dietary Fiber: 1 g
Dietary Exchanges: Vegetable: 1, Bread: 1, Meat: 2½, Fat: 1½

RED SNAPPER SCAMPI

¼ **cup margarine or butter, softened**
1 **tablespoon white wine**
1½ **teaspoons bottled minced garlic**
½ **teaspoon grated lemon peel**
⅛ **teaspoon black pepper**
1½ **pounds red snapper, orange roughy or grouper fillets (about 4 to 5 ounces each)**

1. Preheat oven to 450°F. Combine margarine, wine, garlic, lemon peel and pepper in small bowl; stir to blend.

2. Place fish on foil-lined shallow baking pan. Top with seasoned margarine. Bake 10 to 12 minutes or until fish begins to flake easily when tested with fork.   *Makes 4 servings*

Prep and cook time:
12 minutes

Nutrients per serving: Calories: 278, Total Fat: 14 g, Protein: 35 g, Carbohydrate: 1 g, Cholesterol: 62 mg, Sodium: 208 mg, Dietary Fiber: trace Dietary Exchanges: Meat: 5

Serve It With Style!

You can add sliced carrots, zucchini and bell pepper cut into matchstick-size strips to the baking pan for an easy vegetable side dish. Serve these vegetables and the Red Snapper Scampi over hot steamed white rice to make your meal complete!

EASY EASEL
RECIPES

CHICKEN AND ASPARAGUS STIR-FRY

1 cup uncooked rice
2 tablespoons vegetable oil, divided
1 pound boneless skinless chicken
　　breasts, cut into ½-inch-wide strips
2 medium red bell peppers, cut into thin
　　strips
½ pound fresh asparagus, cut diagonally
　　into 1-inch pieces
½ cup bottled stir-fry sauce

1. Cook rice according to package directions.

2. Heat 1 tablespoon oil in wok or large skillet over medium-high heat until hot. Stir-fry chicken 3 to 4 minutes or until chicken is no longer pink in center. Remove from wok; set aside.

3. Heat remaining 1 tablespoon oil in wok until hot. Stir-fry bell peppers and asparagus 1 minute; reduce heat to medium. Cover and cook 2 minutes or until vegetables are crisp-tender, stirring once or twice.

4. Stir in chicken and sauce; heat through. Serve immediately with rice.

Makes 4 servings

Prep and cook time: 18 minutes

Nutrients per serving:
Calories: 442, Total Fat: 11 g,
Protein: 32 g, Carbohydrate: 53 g,
Cholesterol: 69 mg,
Sodium: 806 mg,
Dietary Fiber: 3 g
Dietary Exchanges: Vegetable: 2,
Bread: 3, Meat: 3

GRILLED SALMON FILLETS, ASPARAGUS AND ONIONS

½ teaspoon paprika, preferably sweet Hungarian

6 salmon fillets (6 to 8 ounces each)

⅓ cup bottled honey-Dijon marinade or barbecue sauce

1 bunch (about 1 pound) fresh asparagus spears, ends trimmed

1 large red or sweet onion, cut into ¼-inch slices

1 tablespoon olive oil

1. Prepare grill for grilling. Sprinkle paprika evenly over salmon fillets. Brush marinade over salmon; let stand at room temperature 15 minutes.

2. Brush asparagus and onion slices with olive oil; season with salt and pepper.

3. Place salmon, skin side down, in center of grid over medium coals. Arrange asparagus spears and onion slices around salmon on grid. Grill salmon and vegetables over covered grill 5 minutes. Turn asparagus and onion slices. Grill 5 to 6 minutes more or until salmon flakes easily when tested with a fork and vegetables are crisp-tender. Separate onion slices into rings; arrange over asparagus.

Makes 6 servings

Prep and cook time:
26 minutes

Nutrients per serving:
Calories: 275, Total Fat: 9 g,
Protein: 36 g, Carbohydrate: 13 g,
Cholesterol: 86 mg,
Sodium: 209 mg,
Dietary Fiber: 1 g
Dietary Exchanges: Vegetable: 2,
Meat: 4

THAI GRILLED CHICKEN

**4 boneless chicken breast halves,
skinned if desired (about
1 ¼ pounds)**
¼ cup soy sauce
2 teaspoons bottled minced garlic
½ teaspoon red pepper flakes
2 tablespoons honey
1 tablespoon fresh lime juice

1. Prepare grill for grilling. Place chicken in shallow dish or plate. Combine soy sauce, garlic and pepper flakes in measuring cup. Pour over chicken, turning to coat. Let stand 10 minutes.

2. Meanwhile, combine honey and lime juice in small bowl until blended; set aside.

3. Place chicken on grid over medium coals; brush with some of marinade remaining in dish. Discard remaining marinade. Grill over covered grill 5 minutes. Brush chicken with half of honey mixture; turn and brush with remaining honey mixture. Grill 5 minutes more or until chicken is cooked through.

Makes 4 servings

Prep and cook time: 25 minutes

SERVING SUGGESTION: *Serve with steamed white rice, Oriental vegetables and fresh fruit salad.*

Nutrients per serving:
Calories: 206, Total Fat: 4 g,
Protein: 32 g, Carbohydrate: 10 g,
Cholesterol: 86 mg,
Sodium: 417 mg,
Dietary Fiber: trace
Dietary Exchanges: Fruit: ½,
Meat: 3

EASY EASEL RECIPES

BROILED SALMON FILLETS WITH LIME SALSA

1½ **pounds fresh salmon fillets, quartered**
½ **cup plus 2 tablespoons lime juice, divided**
 1 **jar chunky green salsa or pico de gallo**
⅓ **cup finely chopped green onions, including tops**
⅓ **cup finely chopped fresh cilantro**

1. Preheat broiler. Place fillets, skin sides up, in large casserole. Pour ½ cup lime juice over fillets; set aside. Lightly spray broiler pan with nonstick cooking spray; set aside.

2. Pour salsa into small bowl; mix in remaining 2 tablespoons lime juice, green onions and cilantro. Set aside.

3. Arrange fillets, skin sides up, on prepared broiler pan. Broil 6 inches from heat 4 to 5 minutes or until skin has begun to brown and char slightly. Remove pan; turn fillets over. Return to broiler 6 to 8 minutes or until fillets have begun to brown and flake easily with fork. Serve immediately with lime salsa.

Makes 4 servings

Prep and cook time: 23 minutes

SERVING SUGGESTION:
Serve with additional salsa, steamed white rice and a fresh green salad.

Nutrients per serving:
Calories: 294, Total Fat: 6 g,
Protein: 33 g, Carbohydrate: 27 g,
Cholesterol: 86 mg,
Sodium: 586 mg,
Dietary Fiber: 1 g
Dietary Exchanges: Fruit: 2,
Meat: 3½

EASY EASEL
RECIPES

GRILLED GINGER CHICKEN WITH PINEAPPLE AND COCONUT RICE

1 can (20 ounces) pineapple rings in juice
1 cup uncooked white rice
1/2 cup sweetened flake coconut
4 boneless skinless chicken breast halves (about 1 1/4 pounds)
1 tablespoon soy sauce
1 teaspoon ground ginger

1. Drain juice from pineapple into glass measure. Reserve 2 tablespoons juice for chicken. Combine remaining juice with enough water to equal 2 cups.

2. Cook and stir rice and coconut in medium saucepan over medium heat 3 to 4 minutes or until lightly browned. Add juice mixture; cover and bring to a boil. Reduce heat to low; cook 15 minutes or until rice is tender and liquid is absorbed.

3. While rice is cooking, combine chicken, reserved juice, soy sauce and ginger in medium bowl; toss well.

4. Grill or broil chicken 6 minutes; turn. Add pineapple to grill or broiler pan. Cook 6 to 8 minutes or until chicken is no longer pink in center, turning pineapple after 3 minutes.

5. Transfer rice to 4 serving plates; serve with chicken and pineapple.

Makes 4 servings

Prep and cook time: 22 minutes

Nutrients per serving: Calories: 469, Total Fat: 7 g, Protein: 36 g, Carbohydrate: 64 g, Cholesterol: 86 mg, Sodium: 338 mg, Dietary Fiber: 2 g
Dietary Exchanges: Fruit: 1 1/2, Bread: 2 1/2, Meat: 3 1/2

DILLED SALMON IN PARCHMENT

2 skinless salmon fillets (4 to 6 ounces each)
2 tablespoons butter or margarine, melted
1 tablespoon lemon juice
1 tablespoon chopped fresh dill
1 tablespoon chopped shallots

1. Preheat oven to 400°F. Cut 2 pieces parchment paper into 12-inch squares; fold squares in half diagonally and cut into half heart shapes. Open parchment; place fish fillet on one side of each heart.

2. Combine butter and lemon juice in small cup; drizzle over fish. Sprinkle with dill, shallots and salt and pepper to taste.

3. Fold parchment hearts in half. Beginning at top of heart, fold edges together,

2 inches at a time. At tip of heart, fold parchment over to seal.

4. Bake fish about 10 minutes or until parchment pouch puffs up. To serve, cut an "X" through top layer of parchment and fold back points to display contents.

Makes 2 servings

Prep and cook time: 20 minutes

Nutrients per serving: Calories: 234, Total Fat: 15 g, Protein: 22 g, Carbohydrate: 2 g, Cholesterol: 88 mg, Sodium: 191 mg, Dietary Fiber: trace
Dietary Exchanges: Meat: 3, Fat: 1½

EASY EASEL RECIPES

MEXICALI CHICKEN STEW

1 package (1.25 ounces) taco seasoning, divided
12 ounces boneless skinless chicken thighs
2 cans (14½ ounces each) stewed tomatoes with onions, celery and green peppers
1 package (9 ounces) frozen green beans
1 package (10 ounces) frozen corn
4 cups tortilla chips

1. Place half of taco seasoning in small bowl. Cut chicken thighs into 1-inch pieces; coat with taco seasoning.

2. Coat large nonstick skillet with nonstick cooking spray. Cook and stir chicken 5 minutes over medium heat. Add tomatoes, beans, corn and remaining taco seasoning; bring to a boil.

Reduce heat to medium-low; simmer 10 minutes. Top with tortilla chips before serving.   *Makes 4 servings*

Prep and cook time: 20 minutes

SERVING SUGGESTION: *Serve nachos along with the stew. Spread some of the tortilla chips on a plate; dot with salsa and sprinkle with cheese. Heat just until melted.*

Nutrients per serving: Calories: 396, Total Fat: 13 g, Protein: 20 g, Carbohydrate: 52 g, Cholesterol: 47 mg, Sodium: 955 mg, Dietary Fiber: 5 g
Dietary Exchanges: Vegetable: 3, Bread: 2, Meat: 2, Fat: 1½

Cook's Notes:
To lighten up this dish, simply substitute boneless skinless chicken breasts for the thighs. Each cup of cooked light meat has 44 less calories and 8 less grams of fat than a cup of dark meat.

EASY EASEL RECIPES

MEDITERRANEAN PASTA

12 ounces uncooked rotini pasta

1 bottle (8 ounces) Italian vinaigrette, divided

1 can (6 ounces) tuna packed in water, drained

3 eggs, hard boiled, peeled and cut into wedges

1 cup frozen green beans, thawed

¼ cup pitted black olives

1. Cook pasta according to package directions; drain.

2. Reserve ¼ cup vinaigrette. Toss pasta with remaining vinaigrette; place on serving platter or on individual plates.

3. Arrange tuna, eggs, green beans and olives on top of pasta. Drizzle with reserved vinaigrette. Serve chilled or at room temperature. *Makes 6 servings*

Prep and cook time: 20 minutes

FOR A SPECIAL TOUCH, GARNISH MEDITERRANEAN PASTA WITH RED PEPPER RING AND FRESH DILL.

Nutrients per serving: Calories: 351, Total Fat: 23 g, Protein: 15 g, Carbohydrate: 22 g, Cholesterol: 115 mg, Sodium: 663 mg, Dietary Fiber: trace
Dietary Exchanges: Vegetable: 1, Meat: 2, Fat: 4½

Serve It With Style!

Serve with an easy, flavor-boosting garnish: parsley-dipped lemon wedges. Place parsley in small bowl and dip cut edge of each lemon wedge into parsley to coat lemon.

REUBEN CHICKEN MELTS

4 boneless skinless chicken breast halves
1 large onion, cut into ½-inch slices
1¼ cups Thousand Island salad dressing, divided
2 cups shredded red cabbage
1½ cups (6 ounces) shredded Swiss cheese
4 French rolls, split

1. Brush chicken and onion with ½ cup salad dressing. Set aside.

2. Combine ¼ cup salad dressing and cabbage; mix well. Set aside.

3. Grill chicken over hot coals 5 to 7 minutes on each side or until no longer pink in center. Sprinkle chicken evenly with Swiss cheese during last minute of grilling. Grill onion 4 to 5 minutes on each side or until browned and tender. Grill rolls until toasted.

4. Spread toasted sides of rolls with remaining ½ cup salad dressing. Place chicken on roll bottoms. Top with onion, cabbage mixture and roll tops. Serve immediately. *Makes 4 servings*

Prep and cook time: 25 minutes

Nutrients per serving: Calories: 720, Total Fat: 44 g, Protein: 42 g, Carbohydrate: 38 g, Cholesterol: 132 mg, Sodium: 957 mg, Dietary Fiber: 4 g
Dietary Exchanges: Vegetable: 1, Bread: 2, Meat: 4, Fat: 7

EASY EASEL RECIPES

TUNA MONTE CRISTO SANDWICHES

4 thin slices (2 ounces) **Cheddar cheese**
4 slices **sour dough or challah (egg) bread**
½ pound **deli tuna salad**
1 **egg, beaten**
¼ cup **milk**
2 tablespoons **butter or margarine**

1. Place 1 slice cheese on each bread slice. Spread tuna salad evenly over two slices of cheese-topped bread. Close sandwiches with remaining bread slices.

2. Combine egg and milk in shallow bowl. Dip sandwiches in egg mixture, turning to coat well.

3. Melt butter in large nonstick skillet over medium heat. Add sandwiches; cook 4 to 5 minutes per side or until bread is golden brown and cheese is melted.

Makes 2 servings

Prep and cook time: 20 minutes

SERVING SUGGESTION: *Serve Tuna Monte Cristo Sandwiches with tortilla chips or potato chips and a chilled fresh fruit salad for dessert.*

Nutrients per serving: Calories: 592, Total Fat: 36 g, Protein: 29 g, Carbohydrate: 38 g, Cholesterol: 207 mg, Sodium: 1146 mg, Dietary Fiber: trace
Dietary Exchanges: Bread: 2½, Meat: 3, Fat: 5½

Cook's Notes:

Challah is a traditional Jewish yeast bread. It is rich with eggs and has an airy texture. Challah can be found in many forms, but the most common shape is braided.

EASY EASEL RECIPES

MUSTARD-GLAZED CHICKEN SANDWICHES

½ **cup honey-mustard barbecue sauce,
    divided**
4 **Kaiser rolls, split**
4 **boneless skinless chicken breast
    halves (1 pound)**
4 **slices Swiss cheese**
4 **leaves leaf lettuce**
8 **slices tomato**

1. Spread about 1 teaspoon barbecue sauce on cut sides of each roll.

2. Pound chicken breast halves between 2 pieces of plastic wrap to ½-inch thickness with flat side of meat mallet or rolling pin. Spread remaining barbecue sauce over chicken.

3. Cook chicken in large nonstick skillet over medium-low heat 5 minutes per side or until no longer pink in center. Remove skillet from heat. Place cheese slices on chicken; let stand 3 minutes to melt.

4. Place lettuce leaves and tomato slices on roll bottoms; top with chicken and roll tops.
Makes 4 servings

Prep and cook time: 19 minutes

SERVING SUGGESTION:
Serve sandwiches with yellow tomatoes, baby carrots and celery sticks.

*Nutrients per serving:
Calories: 464, Total Fat: 14 g,
Protein: 39 g, Carbohydrate:
43 g, Cholesterol: 95 mg,
Sodium: 787 mg,
Dietary Fiber: trace
Dietary Exchanges: Bread: 3,
Meat: 4, Fat: ½*

TUNA SALAD STUFFED RED BELL PEPPERS

2 cans (6 ounces each) albacore tuna packed in water, drained
½ cup (2 ounces) shredded sharp Cheddar cheese
⅓ cup reduced-calorie mayonnaise
2 large ribs celery, sliced diagonally
½ cup green grapes, halved
4 small red bell peppers, halved lengthwise and seeded

Nutrients per serving: Calories: 324, Total Fat: 12 g, Protein: 30 g, Carbohydrate: 25 g, Cholesterol: 55 mg, Sodium: 516 mg, Dietary Fiber: 5 g
Dietary Exchanges: Vegetable: 3, Fruit: ½, Meat: 4

Cook's Notes:

Bell peppers have a mild, sweet flavor and come in varieties such as green, yellow, orange and purple. The red bell pepper is a green bell pepper that has been ripened longer, giving it a sweet flavor.

1. Combine tuna, cheese, mayonnaise, celery and grapes in medium bowl; blend well. Season to taste with salt and black pepper.

2. Divide tuna mixture evenly among bell pepper halves, filling to tops.

Makes 4 servings

Prep time: 20 minutes

CHICKEN PESTO PIZZA

- **8 ounces chicken tenders**
- **1 medium onion, thinly sliced**
- **⅓ cup prepared pesto**
- **3 medium plum tomatoes, thinly sliced**
- **1 prepared pizza crust (14 inches)**
- **1 cup (4 ounces) shredded mozzarella cheese**

1. Preheat oven to 450°F. Cut chicken into bite-size pieces. Coat nonstick skillet with nonstick cooking spray; cook and stir chicken over medium heat 2 minutes. Add onion and pesto; cook and stir about 3 minutes or until chicken is cooked through.

2. Arrange tomatoes and chicken mixture on pizza crust to within 1 inch of edge. Sprinkle with cheese. Bake 8 minutes or until pizza is hot and cheese is melted and bubbly.

Makes 6 servings

Prep and cook time: 22 minutes

Nutrients per serving: Calories: 427, Total Fat: 14 g, Protein: 22 g, Carbohydrate: 51 g, Cholesterol: 36 mg, Sodium: 831 mg, Dietary Fiber: 4 g
Dietary Exchanges: Vegetable: 1, Bread: 3, Meat: 1½, Fat: 2½

Cook's Notes:

Plum tomatoes, also called Italian plum, are small and oval in shape. They are fleshy, full of flavor and come in red and yellow varieties.

EASY EASEL RECIPES

TIC-TAC-TOE TUNA PIZZA

1 **bread-style prepared pizza crust (10 ounces)**

1 **can (12 ounces) tuna packed in water, drained**

½ **cup minced onion**

⅓ **cup reduced-fat mayonnaise**

9 **thin plum tomato slices**

4 to 5 **slices (¾ ounce each) process cheese food or American cheese**

1. Preheat oven to 425°F. Place crust on pizza pan or baking sheet.

2. Combine tuna, onion and mayonnaise in medium bowl; season to taste with salt and pepper. Stir until blended. Spread mixture over crust, leaving 1-inch border. Arrange tomato slices on tuna mixture in 3 rows, spacing at least ½ inch apart.

3. Bake 10 to 12 minutes or until heated through.

4. While pizza is baking, cut cheese slices into ½-inch-wide strips.

5. Remove pizza from oven. Arrange enough cheese strips over tuna mixture to resemble tic-tac-toe game. Crisscross remaining strips over some tomato slices. Let stand 5 minutes before serving. *Makes 6 servings*

Prep and cook time: 30 minutes

Nutrients per serving:
Calories: 296, Total Fat: 10 g,
Protein: 26 g, Carbohydrate: 45 g,
Cholesterol: 18 mg,
Sodium: 635 mg,
Dietary Fiber: trace
Dietary Exchanges: Bread: 2½,
Meat: 2

BLUE CHEESE STUFFED CHICKEN BREASTS

**2 tablespoons margarine or butter,
softened, divided**
½ cup (2 ounces) crumbled blue cheese
¾ teaspoon dried thyme leaves
**2 whole boneless chicken breasts with
skin (not split)**
**1 tablespoon bottled or fresh lemon
juice**
½ teaspoon paprika

1. Prepare grill for grilling. Combine
1 tablespoon margarine, blue cheese and
thyme in small bowl until blended. Season
with salt and pepper.

2. Loosen skin over breast of chicken by
pushing fingers between skin and meat,
taking care not to tear skin. Spread blue
cheese mixture under skin with a rubber
spatula or small spoon; massage skin to
evenly spread cheese mixture.

3. Place chicken, skin side down, on grid
over medium coals. Grill over covered grill
5 minutes. Meanwhile, melt remaining
1 tablespoon margarine; stir in lemon juice
and paprika. Turn chicken; brush with
lemon juice mixture. Grill 5 to 7 minutes
more or until chicken is cooked through.
Transfer chicken to carving board; cut each
breast in half. *Makes 4 servings*

Prep and cook time: 22 minutes

SERVING SUGGESTION: *Serve with steamed
new potatoes and broccoli.*

*Nutrients per serving: Calories: 296, Total Fat: 17 g,
Protein: 32 g, Carbohydrate: 1 g, Cholesterol: 93 mg,
Sodium: 333 mg, Dietary Fiber: trace
Dietary Exchanges: Meat: 4, Fat: 1½*

BROCCOLI-FISH ROLLUPS

1 **can (10¾ ounces) cream of broccoli**
   soup
½ **cup milk**
2 **cups seasoned stuffing crumbs**
¾ **pound flounder (4 medium pieces)**
1 **box (10 ounces) broccoli spears,**
   thawed
   Paprika

1. Preheat oven to 375°F. Grease 9-inch square baking pan. Combine soup and milk in bowl. Set aside ½ cup soup mixture.

2. Combine stuffing crumbs and remaining soup mixture. Pat in prepared pan.

3. Place fish on clean work surface. Arrange 1 broccoli spear across narrow end of fish. Starting at narrow end,

gently roll up fish. Place over stuffing mixture, seam side down. Repeat with remaining fish and broccoli.

4. Arrange any remaining broccoli spears over stuffing mixture. Spoon reserved ½ cup soup mixture over broccoli-fish rollups. Sprinkle with paprika.

5. Bake 20 minutes or until fish flakes easily when tested with fork.   *Makes 4 servings*

Prep and cook time: 30 minutes

Nutrients per serving:
Calories: 198, Total Fat: 4 g,
Protein: 21 g, Carbohydrate: 19 g,
Cholesterol: 51 mg,
Sodium: 650 mg, Dietary Fiber: 3 g
Dietary Exchanges: Vegetable: 1,
Bread: 1, Meat: 2

EASY EASEL RECIPES

CHICKEN AND VEGETABLE PASTA

8 ounces (4 cups) uncooked bow tie pasta

2 red or green bell peppers, seeded and cut into quarters

1 medium zucchini, cut into halves

3 boneless skinless chicken breast halves (about 1 pound)

½ cup Italian dressing

½ cup prepared pesto sauce

1. Cook pasta according to package directions. Drain; place in large bowl. Cover to keep warm.

2. While pasta is cooking, combine vegetables, chicken and dressing in medium bowl; toss well. Grill or broil 6 to 8 minutes on each side or until vegetables are crisp-tender and chicken is no longer pink in center. (Vegetables may take less time than chicken.)

3. Cut vegetables and chicken into bite-sized pieces. Add vegetables, chicken and pesto to pasta; toss well. *Makes 4 to 6 servings*

Prep and cook time: 20 minutes

Nutrients per serving: Calories: 688, Total Fat: 34 g, Protein: 38 g, Carbohydrate: 59 g, Cholesterol: 74 mg, Sodium: 514 mg, Dietary Fiber: 2 g
Dietary Exchanges: Vegetable: 2, Bread: 3½, Meat: 3, Fat: 5

BAKED COD WITH TOMATOES AND OLIVES

1 **pound cod fillets (about 4 fillets), cut into 2-inch-wide pieces**
1 **can (14½ ounces) diced Italian-style tomatoes, drained**
2 **tablespoons chopped pitted ripe olives**
1 **teaspoon bottled minced garlic**
2 **tablespoons chopped fresh parsley**

1. Preheat oven to 400°F. Spray 13×9-inch baking dish with nonstick olive oil cooking spray. Arrange cod fillets in dish; season to taste with salt and pepper.

2. Combine tomatoes, olives and garlic in bowl. Spoon over fish.

3. Bake 20 minutes or until fish flakes easily when tested with fork. Sprinkle with parsley.

Makes 4 servings

Prep and cook time: 25 minutes

Nutrients per serving: Calories: 133, Total Fat: 2 g, Protein: 21 g, Carbohydrate: 5 g, Cholesterol: 48 mg, Sodium: 429 mg, Dietary Fiber: 1 g
Dietary Exchanges: Vegetable: 1, Meat: 2½

Serve It With Style!

For a great accompaniment to this dish, spread French bread with softened butter, sprinkle with paprika and oregano, and broil until lightly toasted.

EASY EASEL RECIPES

PEPPY PESTO TOSS

8 ounces uncooked ziti or mostaccioli
1 package (16 ounces) frozen bell pepper and onion strips, thawed
½ pound deli turkey breast or smoked turkey breast, cut ½ inch thick
1 cup half-and-half
½ cup pesto sauce
¼ cup grated Parmesan or Asiago cheese

1. Cook pasta according to package directions.

2. Add pepper and onion mixture to pasta water during last 2 minutes of cooking. Meanwhile, cut turkey into ½-inch cubes.

3. Drain pasta and vegetables in colander.

4. Combine half-and-half, pesto sauce and turkey in saucepan used to prepare pasta. Cook 2 minutes more or until heated through.

5. Return pasta and vegetables to saucepan and toss well to coat. Sprinkle with grated cheese. Serve immediately.

Makes 4 servings

Prep and cook time: 20 minutes

Nutrients per serving: Calories: 581, Total Fat: 26 g, Protein: 28 g, Carbohydrate: 60 g, Cholesterol: 75 mg, Sodium: 1040 mg, Dietary Fiber: 2 g
Dietary Exchanges: Vegetable: 3, Bread: 3, Meat: 2, Fat: 4

Cook's Notes:
Pesto is an uncooked sauce made with fresh basil, garlic, pine nuts, Parmesan cheese and olive oil. It can be found in most supermarkets in the refrigerated section.

Snappy Seafood

*Baked Cod with Tomatoes
and Olives (page 66)*